SpringerBriefs in Computer Science

SpringerBriefs present concise summaries of cutting-edge research and practical applications across a wide spectrum of fields. Featuring compact volumes of 50 to 125 pages, the series covers a range of content from professional to academic.

Typical topics might include:

- A timely report of state-of-the art analytical techniques
- A bridge between new research results, as published in journal articles, and a contextual literature review
- A snapshot of a hot or emerging topic
- An in-depth case study or clinical example
- A presentation of core concepts that students must understand in order to make independent contributions

Briefs allow authors to present their ideas and readers to absorb them with minimal time investment. Briefs will be published as part of Springer's eBook collection, with millions of users worldwide. In addition, Briefs will be available for individual print and electronic purchase. Briefs are characterized by fast, global electronic dissemination, standard publishing contracts, easy-to-use manuscript preparation and formatting guidelines, and expedited production schedules. We aim for publication 8–12 weeks after acceptance. Both solicited and unsolicited manuscripts are considered for publication in this series.

**Indexing: This series is indexed in Scopus, Ei-Compendex, and zbMATH **

Gulnara Z. Karimova

Humanizing AI
with Personality

 Springer

Gulnara Z. Karimova
School of Business & Economics
Westminster International University
in Tashkent
Tashkent, Uzbekistan

AI Boutique Cloud Inc.
Hamilton, ON, Canada

ISSN 2191-5768 ISSN 2191-5776 (electronic)
SpringerBriefs in Computer Science
ISBN 978-3-031-82326-8 ISBN 978-3-031-82327-5 (eBook)
https://doi.org/10.1007/978-3-031-82327-5

This Springer imprint is published by the registered company Springer Nature Switzerland AG
The registered company address is: Gewerbestrasse 11, 6330 Cham, Switzerland

If disposing of this product, please recycle the paper.

Foreword

Artificial intelligence is getting more integrated into our daily lives and the ways these systems interact with us are evolving. One of the most significant developments in this interaction is the emergence of AI systems with a personality. In other words, AI systems, beyond task execution which is reflected in their unique personas, are now being designed to express unique personalities, providing users more natural, engaging, and human-like experiences. That means we need to focus not only on how AI-enabled systems work but also on the broader societal and ethical aspects of the interaction of intelligent machines with humans which represent the personality traits of the systems.

The book investigates the dimensions of such personality-laden agents, exploring their philosophical perspectives, structural composition, technical design, ethical considerations, and impacts across business.

Based on her deep academic background in human communication, Dr. Karimova represents here a comprehensive overview of the principles, frameworks, and foundations to show how to add a personality layer to the AI systems. She highlights the ethical and behavioral considerations to ensure AI improves our lives without compromising our autonomy and values. The author provides the readers with both the theoretical foundations of AI personality as well as the practical development advice showing the step-by-step process of integrating personality into the AI systems.

At the core of AI personality lies the distinction between persona and personality. The persona of an AI system is the external role that the AI is supposed to play in order to address some specific user needs in a particular context. However, a personality is the consistent internal behavioral pattern that shapes how the AI system interacts with the users and with the outer world. AI systems can adopt different personas to be aligned with the purpose of the system, specific use cases, different operating environments, a range of functionality requirements, and a variety of user needs. These are separate from the core personality traits, like empathy, friendliness, or professionalism, that form the foundation of system interactions.

Developing AI personas involves a systematic approach, guided by various frameworks and structures. These models, such as the Persona Design Framework or the Personality Dimensions Model, help AI developers craft interactions that are both effective and ethically sound. These frameworks emphasize understanding user needs, defining the AI's role, and selecting appropriate traits, tone, and behavior to ensure seamless and meaningful interactions. Moreover, the Ethical AI personality design highlights the importance of transparency, user autonomy, and responsible design, ensuring that AI systems are not only helpful but also trustworthy and fair.

The ethical foundations of AI with personality are equally important. Drawing from philosophical theories like deontology and teleology, the ethical considerations around AI focus on ensuring that AI systems respect human values, avoid emotional manipulation, and operate with fairness and transparency. As AI systems become more capable of mimicking emotional and social behavior, the line between human-AI interaction and manipulation becomes blurred.

In order to provide a broader context for these discussions, it is necessary to pay attention to the concept of an AI Society versus a Society of AI. An AI Society refers to the transformative impact of AI on human life—how AI is reshaping industries, governance, and everyday interactions. On the other hand, the Society of AI discussed in this book is a community of researchers, developers, and policymakers dedicated to advancing AI technologies while ensuring they align with societal values.

By diving deep into these critical topics, we can foster a future where AI enhances human life in ways that are responsible, thoughtful, and respectful of our shared human values.

Ottawa, Canada   Hamid Rahbar
November 2024   President and CEO Enercom Canada
                                                     President Vitesse Reskilling™ Canada
                                                   President Ottawa Talent Institute (OTI)

Contents

1   Introduction 1
      References 4

**2   Developing a Framework for Integrating Chatbots
      with Personality in Organizations** 7
      2.1   Introduction 7
      2.2   Technology Adoption Models 8
            2.2.1   The Technology Acceptance Model (TAM) 8
            2.2.2   The Value-Based Adoption Model (VAM) 9
      2.3   Chatbot Integration Stages 10
            2.3.1   Strategic Alignment 11
            2.3.2   Design and Development 13
            2.3.3   User Experience and Interface 14
            2.3.4   Security and Compliance 14
            2.3.5   Performance Monitoring and Optimization 14
            2.3.6   Employee Training and Support 15
            2.3.7   Change Management 15
      2.4   Summary 15
      References 16

3   Ethical Foundations of AI with Personality 19
      3.1   Introduction 19
      3.2   Deontological Theories 20
      3.3   Teleological Theories 21
      3.4   Subjective Theories 22
      3.5   Case Study 23
            3.5.1   Description 23
            3.5.2   Deontological Ethics Applied to Character.ai 24

3.6   Teleological Utilitarian Analysis of Character.ai   25
        3.6.1   Benefits of Character.ai   25
        3.6.2   Potential Harms of Character.ai   26
        3.6.3   Balancing the Consequences   27
3.7   Subjective Analysis of Character.ai   28
        3.7.1   Bakhtin's Concept of Answerability   28
        3.7.2   Jean-Paul Sartre's Existential Ethics   29
3.8   Summary   30
References   31

4   **Engineering Society of AI: Philosophical Foundations
    and Technological Integration**   33
4.1   Introduction   33
4.2   Towards Society of AI   34
        4.2.1   Internet of Things   34
        4.2.2   Internet of AI Things (IoAIT)   34
        4.2.3   Multi-agent Systems (MAS)   35
        4.2.4   Defining the Society of AI-Powered Things (SoAI)   35
        4.2.5   Social Internet of Things (SIoT)   36
4.3   The Philosophical Imperative for Society of AI   37
4.4   The Ontology of AI Communication: UNIFY Protocol   38
4.5   Traits of Society and Their Reflection in the Society
        of AI-Powered Things   39
4.6   Social Cohesion, Shared Values, and Power Dynamics
        in the Society of AI   41
        4.6.1   Social Cohesion   41
        4.6.2   Shared Values   41
4.7   Unified AI System Integration   42
4.8   Scenario: UNIFY Protocol in Action   42
4.9   Summary   44
References   45

5   **Creating AI Persona**   49
5.1   Introduction   49
5.2   AI Personas Versus AI Personality   50
5.3   Typology of Chatbot Persona Creation Methods   51
        5.3.1   Predefined Personas   51
        5.3.2   Adaptive Personas Based on User Data   52
        5.3.3   Role-Based Personas   53
        5.3.4   Historical or Cultural Personas   53
        5.3.5   Supportive Personas   54
        5.3.6   Machine-Learned Personalized Personas   55
        5.3.7   Archetype-Based Personas   55
5.4   Summary   56
References   57

**6 Designing the Appearance of Conversational Agents
with Personality** 61
   6.1   Introduction 61
   6.2   A Unified Framework for Crafting Chatbot Personalities 63
   6.3   Defining the Personality Foundation 65
   6.4   Engaging Stakeholders 67
   6.5   Crafting Appearance and Social Presence 69
   6.6   Designing Affective and Emotional Dimensions 71
   6.7   Iterative Development and Feedback Loops 73
   6.8   Summary 74
   References 74

Conclusion 79

Index 81

About the Author

Dr. Gulnara Z. Karimova is a scholar and practitioner at the intersection of marketing communications and artificial intelligence (AI). She holds a Ph.D. in Communications and Media Studies from a QS-ranked university in Cyprus and is currently advancing her expertise through an M.Sc. in Mathematics and Computer Science at Heriot-Watt University. Her career spans over a decade, encompassing consultancy, academia, and entrepreneurial ventures.

As the CEO and product designer at AI Boutique Cloud Inc., a Canadian startup, Dr. Karimova specializes in creating AI-driven chatbots that resonate with client brand identities. Her professional milieu includes extensive consultancy experience across the B2B sector, with a particular focus on AI integration and data science applications in marketing. Her academic contributions are equally noteworthy, with a strong publication record featuring works in esteemed journals such as the *International Journal of Human-Computer Interaction*, the *Journal of Marketing Communications,* and *Journal of Consumer Marketing.*

List of Figures

Fig. 2.1   Key factors influencing the adoption of AI with Personality.
         Note The figure was created using Leonardo.ai and Canva 10
Fig. 2.2   Enhancing brand identity through AI with personality. *Note*
         The figure was created using Canva 11
Fig. 2.3   Chatbot integration stages 12
Fig. 3.1   The diagrammatic representation of deontological
         theories of ethics. *Note* The figure was created using whimsical
         diagrams 21
Fig. 3.2   The diagrammatic representation of teleological
         theories of ethics. *Note* The figure was created using whimsical
         diagrams 22
Fig. 3.3   The diagrammatic representation of subjective
         theories of ethics. *Note* The figure was created using whimsical
         diagrams 23
Fig. 4.1   Diagrammatic representation of an AI
         orchestration framework 43
Fig. 5.1   The typology of chatbot persona. *Note* The figure was created
         using Dall-E and Canva 51
Fig. 6.1   Chatbot Personality Framework. *Note* The figure was created
         using Whimsical Diagrams 66
Fig. 6.2   Key Stakeholders for Chatbot Creation. *Note* The figure
         was created using DALL-E, Pixelcut, and Canva 67
Fig. 6.3   Potential Contributors to the Aesthetic Overshadowing
         in Chatbots. *Note* The figure was created using DALL-E,
         Microsoft Photos, and Canva 71
Fig. 6.4   Stages of Emotional Growth in AI Chatbots. *Note* The figure
         was created using DALL-E, Microsoft Photos, and Canva 72

List of Figures

List of Tables

Table 4.1   Basic societal traits identified by some key scholars   40
Table 4.2   Key aspects of AI interactions in UNIFY protocol scenario   43

Chapter 1
Introduction

Abstract This book examines the emergence with personality, where conversational agents adopt crafted traits that extend beyond rote function, mimicking qualities that engage the human psyche. This phenomenon is dissected as a confluence of engineering, ethical theory, and philosophical inquiry, scrutinizing the latent impact on human autonomy, cognitive boundaries, and the broader social structure. Through exploration of theoretical models, technical rigor, and the ethical architecture behind personality in AI, the text provides a critical inquiry into how these constructs embed themselves into the contours of contemporary existence, spanning realms of commerce, design, branding, and moral philosophy.

Keywords AI personas · Anthropomorphism · Business integration · Conversational agents · Chatbots · Ethical frameworks · Identity in AI · Moral responsibility · Philosophical foundations · Psychological frameworks · Society of AI-powered things (SoAI) · Social dynamics · User interaction design

Conversational agents and chatbots entered the routines of our existence, bringing into it further convenience through round-the-clock assistance and concurrent handling of enquiries. These digital companions, though fundamentally utilitarian, epitomize a drastic change in our relations with technology. Now, add to that, granting these artificial beings with personality traits. We are not just adding some charm to cold circuits. We are infusing AI with engaging personalities, making our exchanges with them feel as warm and relatable as catching up with an old friend. AI with personality refers to artificial intelligence systems that are instilled with distinct, human-like traits or characteristics, which shape how they interact with users. The idea of AI systems having personality is not new and can be traced back to earlier studies on designing product personality [6]. Personality can be described as a person's dynamic and structured set of non-physical traits that distinctly shape their thoughts, emotions, and behaviors across different situations [12] and give both "consistency and individuality to a person's behavior" [4]. The AI systems can be designed to convey a particular persona or character—such as being friendly, professional, humorous, or authoritative—through their tone, language, and behavior [11].

For instance, archetype-based personas, drawn from Jungian archetypes like the Hero, the Caregiver, or the Explorer, breathe life into AI, making them capable of sparking bravery, offering solace, and fuelling our curiosity. This is not just about boosting AI intelligence—it is about giving them the knack for emotional resonance and winning our trust [8].

This transformation prompts an exploration of the ramifications of these changes on the nature of relations between humans and their digital counterparts. This change would also affect business environments demanding close attention to the process of integration of chatbots with personalities into organizations.

Blending scientific precision with philosophical perception, each chapter of this book systematically addresses the stages and phases of this integration, providing a comprehensive guide for organizations. Despite the abundance of frameworks that focus on technology integration, a significant gap persists regarding the incorporation of chatbots with distinct personalities. Existing models, such as the Technology Acceptance Model (TAM) [2] and its extensions, emphasis factors influencing technology adoption, often overlooking the specifics involved in deploying chatbots with personas. The absence of a dedicated framework for these advanced chatbots reveals the need for a new model.

The book begins by establishing a foundational framework for integrating AI with personality traits into business contexts, where I provide implementation strategies. It then examines the ethical implications of giving machines human-like characteristics, featuring my analysis of the associated moral dilemmas and societal impacts. Next, it explores the societal effects of AI on social interactions and norms, incorporating my research on the transformation of social dynamics. Subsequently, it presents a detailed classification of AI personas and methodologies for creating these archetypes, including my original contribution on AI archetypes. This cohesive structure equips practitioners with the insights needed for developing effective AI-driven solutions. Finally, the book provides a practical synthesis, illustrating how the personality-grounded framework can be applied in real-world contexts. It addresses the challenge of aligning the varied perspectives and interests of stakeholders to shape conversational agents that reflect carefully constructed personalities.

Indeed, further humanization of conversational AI-powered agents transforms the modes of relation between humans and their digital counterparts. The relationship between humans and AI-powered technology can be depicted by two contrasting modes of interaction. On one end, there is a harmonious and mutually beneficial partnership. In this scenario, AI and humans collaborate to create novel expressions and innovations that neither could achieve independently. Such "poietic symbiosis" [9, 10] infers that both parties expand each other's capabilities.

On the other hand, a detrimental relationship can emerge, defined as "algorithmic subjugation" [9, 10]. In this paradigm, the relationship between AI and humans shifts towards exploitation and suppression. Humans are reduced to mere data sources, and their contributions are instrumentalized to refine AI systems, leading to a scenario where humans are subsumed by the very technology they created. A scenario of a "machinic enslavement," [3] every keystroke and click are harnessed for the data-driven whims of digital lords and the tool has become the master. AI, once our humble servant, now directs human lives like a digital despot, dictating the terms of engagement.

This technological ascendance reveals the dependencies between AI systems and domain expertise. Every algorithmic decision reflects the understanding of human experts. The precise knowledge imparted by auditors, for example, serves as the criterion for algorithms that automatically assign accounts. Such interactions show the indispensable role of human intelligence in refining AI capabilities while at the same time demonstrating the dominance of these technological entities. The lamentation of developers, who wish to infuse the intelligence of the auditors into artificial intelligence, reflects the paradox of AI's rise: a tool designed to augment human capacity now stands as an autonomous entity dictating its own operational directives. Humans, by feeding AI with their knowledge, effectively become the resource or feeding material for these systems.

One must recognize that neither the charming partnership of poietic symbiosis nor the rigid control of algorithmic domination spares humans from surveillance. In a poietic symbiosis, AI and humans partake in a collaboration that, while enhancing creativity, subtly incorporates mechanisms for continuous monitoring and data collection. This form of surveillance, particularly evident in the realm of social media, possesses an "entertaining side" [1], suggesting that the allure of AI might obscure its ramifications for privacy. In a scenario of algorithmic subjugation, humans find themselves subordinate to AI systems, with their every action tracked to optimize AI performance. This subtle surveillance represents a paradigm shift where human agency and creativity are under constant scrutiny. Hence, the integration of AI tools across various domains signifies not only a new mode of interaction but also introduces new forms of surveillance [5].

Transitioning from this omnipresent oversight to a more thoughtful comprehension of human–machine interaction, the polyphonic model presents a strikingly connected web. In this polyphonic framework, we find ourselves entangled in a dense network of interactions, where the distinctions between creator and tool, self and other, become obscured. This interconnectedness is a continuous process of mutual transformation and evolution. Humans and AI co-create and co-evolve, their relationship is a dynamic cycle [9, 10]. AI absorbs the insights of human knowledge, while humans adapt to the emergent intelligence of AI, perpetually reshaping one another in a dialogic relationship. That is why the choices we make in AI development are not simply technical decisions,they are profoundly human ones, shaping both our technologies and ourselves. Given the mutual influence of humans and AI, it becomes essential to deepen our understanding of what it means to build a society with AI as an active participant.

The concept of Society of AI demands that we get to the heart of what makes a society, by examining its defining traits. Typically, societies are human constructs, built on a web of interactions and shared values. But can we stretch this idea to include AI? Indeed, objects in a society of things can be considered entities, complete with identities and the ability to communicate [7]. Following this line of thought, AI can be considered capable of being part of society because, like humans, AI entities can exhibit communication, social cohesion, shared values, and ethical standards [7].

At first glance, the endeavor to sculpt a conversational agent's persona might seem elusive, an ephemeral chase analogous to capturing the essence of wind in a jar. Yet, beneath this abstraction lies a very real arsenal of stimuli—visual, auditory, and linguistic—that collectively transcend functionality. A chatbot doesn't simply speak; it resonates, much like a finely tuned instrument whose tone, rhythm, and cadence induce impressions far beyond the words themselves.

And just as the voice can shape impressions, so too can the chatbot's appearance—though devoid of physicality—carry the burden of its constructed identity. Here—whether through an avatar, a sheer text interface, or something more elaborate,—the design must walk a fine line. The risk emerges when the design becomes overengineered, where attention to visual detail overwhelms the very function the chatbot is meant to serve. This is where the phenomenon of aesthetic overshadowing occurs, much like an ornate frame that distracts from the painting it encloses. When too much focus is placed on visual perfection, the chatbot teeters on the edge of the uncanny valley, evoking discomfort rather than trust. Yet, if too little care is given, the bot may devolve into a sterile, mechanical entity, lacking the warmth needed for true connection.

But beyond visual and auditory refinement lies the deeper process through which the chatbot's persona truly emerges—emotional ontogeny. Unlike static, preprogrammed entities, these chatbots adapt, learning to read and respond to the subtle cues of human emotions over time. Much like a young child developing social awareness, the chatbot refines its emotional responses through interactions, adjusting its tone and behavior in ways that evoke empathy or mitigate frustration. This iterative process allows the chatbot to move beyond simple mechanical responses, converting it into a more lifelike conversational interlocuter, capable of sensing and modulating its emotional tone to suit the context. It is here, within the layers of adaptation, where the design of the chatbot undergoes its true evolution, mutating and sharpening its responses with each new encounter.

References

1. Albrechtslund, A., Dubbeld, L.: The entertaining side of surveillance. Surveill. Soc. **3**(2/3), 216–221 (2005)
2. Davis, F.D.: Perceived usefulness, perceived ease of use, and user acceptance of information technology. MIS Q. **13**(3), 319–340 (1989)
3. Deleuze, G., Guattari, F.: Anti-Oedipus: Capitalism and Schizophrenia. University of Minnesota Press (1983)
4. Feist, J., Feist, G.J.: Theories of Personality, 6th edn. McGraw-Hill, New York (2008)
5. Galič, M., Timan, T., Koops, B.J.: Bentham, Deleuze and beyond: an overview of surveillance theories from the panopticon to participation. Philosophy and Technol **30**(1), 9–37 (2017). https://doi.org/10.1007/s13347-016-0219-1
6. Janlert, L.E., Stolterman, E.: The character of things. Des. Stud. **18**(3), 297–314 (1997)
7. Karimova, G.Z., Shirkhanbeik, A.: Society of things: An alternative vision of the Internet of things. Cogent Soc. Sci. **1**(1), (2016). https://doi.org/10.1080/23311886.2015.1115654

8. Karimova, G.Z., Goby, V.P.: The adaptation of anthropomorphism and archetypes for marketing artificial intelligence. J. Consum. Mark. **38**(2), 229–238 (2021). https://doi.org/10.1108/JCM-04-2020-3785

9. Karimova, G.Z., Kim, Y.D., Shirkhanbeik.: A. Poietic symbiosis or algorithmic subjugation: generative AI technology in marketing communications education. Educ. Inf. Technol. (2024) https://doi.org/10.1007/s10639-024-12877-8

10. Karimova, G.Z.: The dialogic evolution of ai-based products: a polyphonic analysis of temporal transformations. Int. J. Human–Comput. Interact. (2024)

11. Lee, K.M., Peng, W., Jin, S.-A., Yan, C.: Can robots manifest personality? An empirical test of personality recognition, social responses, and social presence in human–robot interaction. J. Commun. **56**(4), 754–772 (2006). https://doi.org/10.1111/j.1460-2466.2006.00318.x

12. Ryckman, R.: Theories of Personality . Thomson/Wadsworth (2004)

Chapter 2
Developing a Framework for Integrating Chatbots with Personality in Organizations

Abstract This chapter presents a framework for integrating chatbots with well-defined personalities into organizational settings, emphasizing their role in enhancing customer engagement, operational efficiency, and brand consistency. Existing models, such as the Technology Acceptance Model (TAM) and its expansions are reviewed. However, a significant gap in the literature is identified, as current frameworks primarily address standard chatbots and fail to accommodate the complexities of those with personalities. The proposed framework addresses this gap by describing the specific requirements and stages for integrating personality-driven chatbots. It encompasses strategic alignment with business objectives, persona development reflecting brand identity, and advanced natural language processing (NLP) and machine learning techniques for adaptive interactions. Integration with existing systems, user experience design, security and compliance, performance monitoring, and continuous improvement processes are also detailed. This chapter provides a step-by-step guide for organizations to effectively implement chatbots with personalities to elevate user involvement, improve operational efficiency, and establish a consistent, impactful brand presence.

Keywords Artificial intelligence · Branding · Human-AI interaction · Personality · Technology integration

2.1 Introduction

Chatbots are becoming the charismatic front-liners of customer communication. They boost operational efficiency, polish the brand's image to a shine, and, when endowed with well-defined personalities, offer a treasure trove of advantages. These charming digital entities build deeper connections with users, deliver personalized interactions that make customers feel special, cut operational costs [1], and augment brand identity with every conversation. It is no wonder personality-driven chatbots are hailed as invaluable assets for any organization striving to stand out [8].

© The Author(s), under exclusive license to Springer Nature Switzerland AG 2025
G. Z. Karimova, *Humanizing AI with Personality*,
SpringerBriefs in Computer Science, https://doi.org/10.1007/978-3-031-82327-5_2

Implementation of AI with personality requires a systematic approach covering multiple stages: strategic alignment, persona development, system integration, user experience design, security protocols, performance monitoring, training, and change management. These phases establish that the technology corresponds with organizational goals, develops relatable AI personalities, integrates smoothly into existing systems, prioritizes user needs, defends sensitive data, maintains optimal performance, equips staff, and manages organizational shifts.

However, before initiating chatbot implementation, confirming that the technology will be readily accepted by users is vital. Therefore, identifying and understanding the specific factors that facilitate user adoption will directly influence technology's integration and effectiveness.

2.2   Technology Adoption Models

Frameworks that address every aspect—from strategic alignment to technical integration—are indispensable for guiding the systematic adoption of such chatbots. Many studies on the use of innovative products are grounded on the Technology Acceptance Model (TAM), Theory of Planned Behavior (TPB), and Unified Theory of Acceptance and Use of Technology (UTAUT) [9]. By incorporating insights from these models, organizations can accelerate AI adoption rates and maximize the technology's impact.

2.2.1   The Technology Acceptance Model (TAM)

The technology acceptance model (TAM) is widely used in management literature to describe how technology adoption occurs in a firm [5]. Developed by Fred Davis in 1989, TAM puts forward two primary factors that influence technology adoption: perceived usefulness (PU) and perceived ease of use (PEOU) (ibid). Perceived usefulness refers to the degree to which a person believes that using a particular system would refine their job performance, while perceived ease of use refers to the degree to which a person believes that using the system would be free of effort.

TAM has been widely adopted and extended in various contexts to explain the adoption of different technologies. [21] proposed an extended version known as TAM2, which incorporates additional determinants such as social influence processes (subjective norms) and cognitive instrumental processes (job relevance, output quality, and result demonstrability) [21]. These extensions help in understanding the broader range of factors influencing technology acceptance.

Subsequent research has continued to expand TAM, incorporating elements like trust, compatibility, and facilitating conditions. For example [22] developed the

Unified Theory of Acceptance and Use of Technology (UTAUT), which synthesizes TAM with other models to include factors such as facilitating conditions and social influence, providing a more comprehensive framework [22].

In the context of AI chatbots [23] extended TAM by adding factors specifically relevant to AI adoption, such as subjective norms, compatibility, facilitating conditions, and trust. These additions reflect the evolving nature of technology acceptance and the need to consider a wider range of influences in modern technological environments [23].

2.2.2 The Value-Based Adoption Model (VAM)

However, for AI-based intelligent products, the value-based adoption model (VAM) was found to surpass other prevalent models, such as TAM, TPB, and UTAUT, in accuracy [20]. Employing a methodology initially developed for advanced driver assistance systems [18], the study by [20] reveals that the VAM model not only incorporates the fundamental attributes of recognized technology acceptance frameworks—specifically, usefulness and technical aspects—but also includes elements of enjoyment and perceived cost [13]. Furthermore, the VAM positions perceived value as a pivotal mediating factor in the decision-making process.

According to [15], the users' intention to adopt artificial intelligence-based chatbots is affected by attitude, perceived usefulness, and trust.

However, a significant lacuna exists in the current literature. Existing frameworks predominantly cater to the integration of standard, functional chatbots, often neglecting the complexities associated with personality-driven interactions. The unique requirements of chatbots with personalities—such as maintaining consistent interactions—demand a new, comprehensive model that addresses these specific challenges.

Chatbots with personalities require a separate framework due to their advanced interaction capabilities and the need for consistent persona management. Unlike standard chatbots, which primarily handle transactional interactions, personality-driven chatbots must sustain engaging, human-like conversations, which involves advanced natural language processing, and adaptive learning algorithms.

Effectively adopting AI with personality requires addressing several key factors (Fig. 2.1). Trust and privacy are paramount, as securing personal data builds confidence among users. AI's usability and responsiveness determine its ability to interact efficiently and meet user expectations. The AI must adjust its interactions according to the user's preferences and behavioral patterns. The personality it conveys should naturally fit the specific context of each interaction. Performance expectations involve the user's belief that the AI will fulfill its designated roles competently. Additionally, the perceived value of the AI reflects how users balance its cost against the benefits it provides. The Technology Acceptance Model (TAM) emphasizes that users believe AI with personality will sharpen performance or simplify tasks, particularly

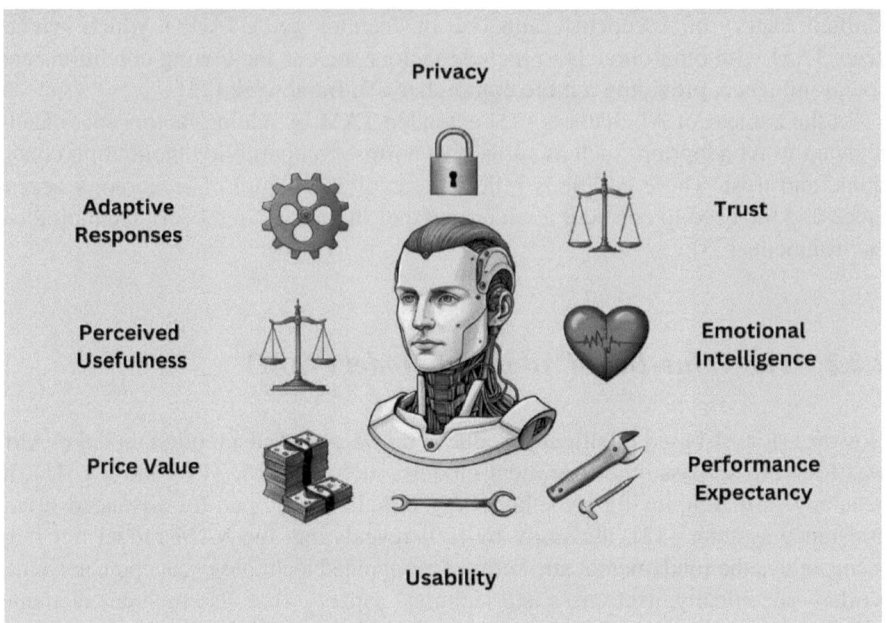

Fig. 2.1 Key factors influencing the adoption of AI with Personality. *Note* The figure was created using Leonardo.ai and Canva

by offering timely and contextually appropriate interactions that resonate with the user's expectations and the organization's brand identity [17].

These factors jointly influence the likelihood of successful adoption of personality-driven AI.

Further, rolling up our sleeves, we move beyond the broad strokes of technology adaptation models, and provide a practical, step-by-step framework for successful AI implementation. The subsequent sections of the chapter will look at each phase of the suggested framework, including strategic alignment, persona development, system integration, user experience, security, performance monitoring, training, and change management.

2.3 Chatbot Integration Stages

Integrating chatbots into an organization requires a strategic approach that begins with aligning the chatbot's functionality with the overarching business goals (Fig. 2.3.). Whether the goal is to elevate customer service, optimize operations, or drive sales, the chatbot must be crafted to align impeccably with these ambitions, making it essential to identify the core users—whether they are customers or employees. By adjusting the chatbot's persona and functionality to resonate with the specific needs and preferences of these users, interactions can be designed to remain meaningful and impactful.

2.3.1   Strategic Alignment

Frontline service employees convey brand meaning to consumers on a one-to-one basis [3, 10]. Correspondence between customer service employees and other brand-related concepts may significantly impact consumers' brand attitudes and purchase intentions [19, 24]. Chatbot interactions, aligned with a company's brand, can significantly improve consumer satisfaction, affective attachment, and purchase intention [14]. Though AI, as a modern service worker, lacks the heartbeat and soul of its human counterparts, it cunningly triggers our social reflexes, making us engage with it as if it were alive [6]. This curious phenomenon invites us to ponder how AI endowed with personality can be used to amplify brand identity.

Using the Kapferer Brand Identity Prism framework, we can integrate advanced AI capabilities across all dimensions to create a unified brand narrative (Fig. 2.2). Kapferer[11] presents six key facets of the Brand Identity Prism: physique, personality, culture, relationship, reflection, and self-image.

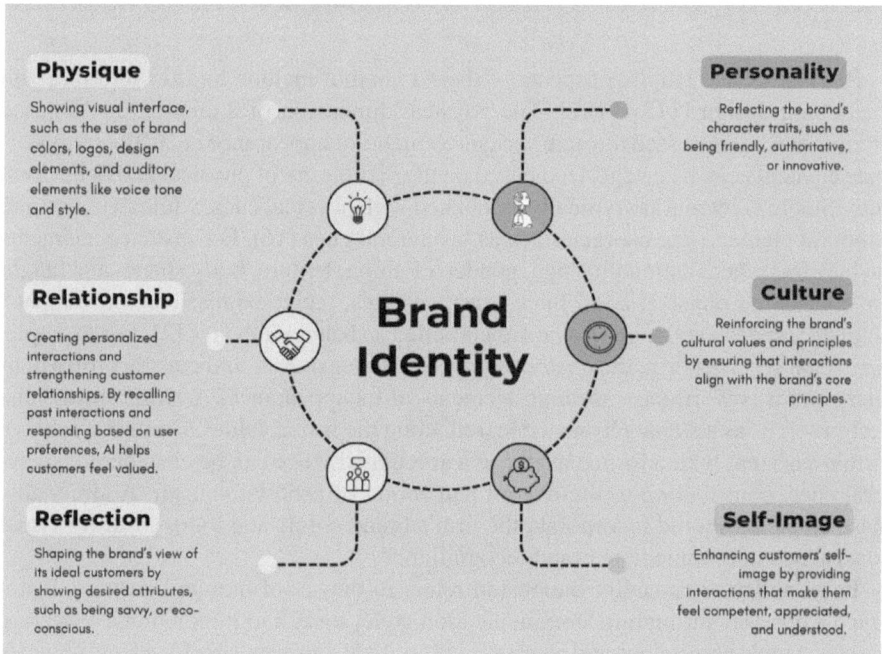

Fig. 2.2   Enhancing brand identity through AI with personality. *Note* The figure was created using Canva

Fig. 2.3 Chatbot integration stages

Physique: The tangible aspects of the AI chatbot include its user interface and interaction design [11, p. 182]. The physical dimension of a chatbot or AI-based product can be expressed through various elements of appearance [12]. These appearance elements can be categorized based on the dichotomy of physical and behavioral cues. Stable elements are typically associated with physical cues, while dynamic and temporal elements are characterized as behavioral cues [16]. For instance, elements such as fragrance, nationality, age, gender, clothing, texture, body shape, and height are considered physical cues. In contrast, gestures, facial expressions, movements, language, speech style, and voice are classified as behavioral cues [2]. For example, for a legal services firm, the chatbot's physical dimension should convey professionalism and trustworthiness through elements of its appearance. A clean, minimalist design serves as a stable physical cue, reflecting the firm's values. Features such as a virtual assistant with a formal avatar or a articulated voice can be considered behavioral cues, contributing to the overall perception of professionalism. Additionally, these elements should incorporate the firm's brand colors and logo, ensuring visual consistency and immediate brand recognition.

Personality: Personality dimension refers to the set of human-like traits that a brand expresses through its communication style, tone, and interactions, reflecting the company's core values and character [11, p. 183]. For instance, for a legal services firm, the chatbot's personality should be crafted to align with these values, conveying professionalism and trustworthiness.

To develop this personality, the chatbot can utilize advanced language processing techniques to converse with clients in a way that feels genuine and professional. This involves responding to client concerns with appropriate empathy and expertise, making the chatbot feel like a reliable guide. For example, the chatbot should maintain a tone that is empathetic, knowledgeable, and confident, reflecting the firm's dedication to client care and legal expertise.

One method to shape this personality is by using specific character types known as archetypes. For instance, the Caregiver and Everyman archetypes, which underline traits such as compassion, approachability, and reliability, can serve as inspiration for the chatbot's design [12]. These archetypes can be reflected through features like a calm and confident tone, direct eye contact in visual elements, and a communication style that is friendly yet professional.

Culture: The chatbot should embody the firm's cultural values, such as commitment to justice, integrity, and client confidentiality [11, p. 184]. Through its responses and interactions, it reflects these values, with each exchange reaffirming the firm's commitment to ethical practices and client-centered service. The cultural alignment between the chatbot's behavior and the firm's values can strengthen client trust and loyalty.

Relationship: The relationship dimension focuses on how the brand interacts with its clients [11, p. 185]. An AI chatbot with a strong personality can evoke a sense of personalized service, making clients feel valued and understood. For instance, the chatbot can remember previous interactions, tailor its responses based on the client's history, and provide timely updates on legal matters. This cultivates a continuous and evolving relationship that elevates client satisfaction and involvement.

Reflection: The reflection dimension concerns how clients perceive themselves when interacting with the brand [11, p. 186]. By engaging in a innovative AI chatbot, clients may view themselves as being associated with a forward-thinking, technologically advanced firm. This perception can increase their confidence in the firm's capabilities and their overall satisfaction with the service.

Self-Image: The self-image dimension relates to how clients aspire to be seen [11, p. 187]. A chatbot with a carefully designed personality can engage clients in a manner that is consistent with the brand's image, enhancing the client's overall experience and satisfaction. This approach helps to reinforce the brand's identity and makes interactions more relatable and memorable for users.

2.3.2 Design and Development

The development stage of a chatbot involves several critical elements, including robust Natural Language Processing (NLP) tools, advanced machine learning models, integration with Customer Relationship Management (CRM) systems, and the use of Application Programming Interfaces (APIs). NLP tools and advanced machine learning models grant the chatbot the ability to understand and respond accurately to user inputs. This adaptability helps create a more personalized user experience. Integrating the chatbot with CRM systems and databases enables the chatbot to draw upon and apply detailed user data adeptly. Utilizing APIs to connect the chatbot with various enterprise systems, third-party services, and emotional AI modules enhances its functionality. The complexity of integration is higher for chatbots with personality due to the need for detailed user data to tailor interactions based on user preferences and past interactions.

2.3.3 User Experience and Interface

Designing the chatbot to operate across multiple platforms, such as websites, mobile apps, and social media, permits users to interact with it wherever they prefer. Focusing on intuitive interfaces and interaction flows helps create a unique user experience. Implementing mechanisms to gather user feedback to refine the chatbot. The user interface for chatbots with personality should support dynamic and engaging interactions, often requiring more sophisticated design elements.

2.3.4 Security and Compliance

Complying with data privacy regulations and implementing vigorous security measures will protect user data and maintain trust, especially for chatbots with personality. Recent advancements have introduced innovative approaches to strengthen security and privacy for AI chatbots. These include multi-factor authentication (MFA) and biometric authentication [7], such as facial recognition and voiceprints. AI-driven threat detection and response systems have been developed to continuously monitor and analyze user behavior, quickly identifying and addressing potential security threats.

For example, in the context of e-health services, the Pryv privacy-compliant stream-based database allows users to control their personal data [4]. The integration of multi-agent systems (MAS) within frameworks like EREBOTS facilitates secure interactions between different agents, such as user agents and doctor agents [4]. By incorporating these security measures and privacy-focused platforms, companies can guarantee their chatbots with personality operate within a secure framework.

2.3.5 Performance Monitoring and Optimization

Defining key performance indicators (KPIs) and using analytics tools to monitor effectiveness are essential for accurately assessing the chatbot's performance and making data-driven improvements. Establishing processes for ongoing learning based on user feedback keeps the chatbot effective and relevant by continually adapting to user needs. Performance metrics for chatbots with personality should include user engagement, satisfaction levels, and the chatbot's ability to adapt its responses to user behavior. These metrics provide essential indicators of success by measuring how well the chatbot interacts with users and maintains or adjusts its persona. Additionally, utilizing sentiment analysis and tracking task completion rates can further help evaluate the chatbot's overall effectiveness.

2.3.6 Employee Training and Support

Developing comprehensive training programs for employees on chatbot usage and management equips them with the skills to operate and troubleshoot the system efficiently. Training should cover the details of managing a chatbot with personality, including techniques for maintaining consistency in persona traits. This training is distinct from standard chatbot training, as it emphasizes techniques for ensuring the chatbot's personality remains aligned with brand identity across various interactions. The training should cover the chatbot's functionalities and provide employees with guidelines on how to manage and adjust its responses to different user types while preserving its established persona.

2.3.7 Change Management

Involving stakeholders throughout the integration process builds engagement and supports smooth implementation. Informing employees and customers about the chatbot's capabilities and benefits helps manage expectations. Communication should focus on the added value of a chatbot with personality and show its potential to increase user participation and strengthen brand loyalty.

2.4 Summary

This chapter offers a detailed framework for integrating chatbots with personalities into organizational environments. It addresses a significant gap in existing technology adoption models, which generally overlook the specific requirements of chatbots with personality-driven capabilities. The chapter builds upon established models, such as the Technology Acceptance Model (TAM) and the Value-Based Adoption Model (VAM), to create an approach that specifically considers chatbots designed to engage users on an emotional level.

The strategic alignment of the chatbot with the organization's goals is the cornerstone of this framework. The chatbot is not just a functional tool but a reflection of the brand itself. For instance, using the Kapferer Brand Identity Prism, the chapter illustrates how the chatbot's persona should align with the company's core values and attributes across various dimensions like physique, personality, culture, relationship, reflection, and self-image. Every interaction the chatbot has with a customer should reinforce the brand's identity and help build a deeper connection with the user.

Security and compliance are given significant attention, especially in the context of handling sensitive personal data. The chapter suggests implementing multi-factor authentication and AI-driven threat detection systems to protect user information.

The framework also outlines the technical stages required for successful integration, such as the use of advanced Natural Language Processing (NLP) tools and machine learning algorithms. These technologies refine the chatbot's capacity to participate in meaningful, human-like conversations consistent with the brand's core concept. The chapter further emphasizes the importance of integrating the chatbot with existing Customer Relationship Management (CRM) systems. In this way, the chatbot can tailor its responses based on each customer's history and preferences, making conversation more personalized.

The chapter provides a comprehensive guide for organizations aiming to implement chatbots that do more than perform basic tasks. These chatbots, when integrated according to the proposed framework, become extensions of the brand, increasing user engagement, operational efficiency, and overall brand loyalty through consistent and emotionally resonant interactions. The detailed focus on strategic alignment, technical integration, and security considerations makes this framework an essential tool for any organization looking to use chatbots as a core element of their branding strategy.

References

1. Adam, M., Wessel, M., Benlian, A.: AI-based chatbots in customer service and their effects on user compliance. Electron. Mark. **31**(2), 427–445 (2021). https://doi.org/10.1007/s12525-020-00414-7
2. Adolphs, R.: Social cognition and the human brain. Trends Cogn. Sci. **3**(12), 469–479 (1999). https://doi.org/10.1016/S1364-6613(99)01399-6
3. Baker, T.L., Rapp, A., Meyer, T., Mullins, R.: The role of brand communications on front line service employee beliefs, behaviours, and performance. J. Acad. Mark. Sci. **42**(6), 642–657 (2014). https://doi.org/10.1007/s11747-014-0376-7
4. Calvaresi, D., Calbimonte, J.-P., Siboni, E., Eggenschwiler, S., Manzo, G., Hilfiker, R., Schumacher, M.: EREBOTS: privacy-compliant agent-based platform for multi-scenario personalized health-assistant chatbots. Electronics **10**(6), 666 (2021). https://doi.org/10.3390/electronics10060666
5. Davis, F.D.: Perceived usefulness, perceived ease of use, and user acceptance of (1989) information technology. MIS Quarterly, **13**(3), 319–340 (1989). https://doi.org/10.2307/249008
6. Desideri, L., Ottaviani, C., Malavasi, M., Di Marzio, R., Bonifacci, P.: Emotional processes in human-robot interaction during brief cognitive testing. Comput. Human. Behav. **90**(January 2019), 331–342 (2019). https://doi.org/10.1016/j.chb.2018.08.013
7. Feng, Q., He, D., Zeadally, S., Wang, H.: Anonymous biometrics-based authentication scheme with key distribution for mobile multi-server environment. Future Generat. Comput. Syst. **84**(July 2018), 239–251 (2018). https://doi.org/10.1016/j.future.2017.07.040

8. Ferraro, C., Demsar, V., Sands, S., Restrepo, M., Campbell, C.: The paradoxes of generative AI enabled customer service: a guide for managers. Bus. Horiz. **67**(5), 1–11 (2024). https://doi.org/10.1016/j.bushor.2024.04.013

9. Groß, M.: Mobile shopping: a classification framework and literature review. Int. J. Retail & Distrib. Manage. **43**(3), 221–241 (2015). https://doi.org/10.1108/IJRDM-06-2013-0119

10. Henkel, S., Tomczak, T., Heitmann, M., Herrmann, A.: Managing brand consistent employee behaviour: relevance and managerial control of behavioural branding. J. Product Brand Manage. **16**(5), 310–320 (2007). https://doi.org/10.1108/10610420710779609

11. Kapferer, J.-N.: The New Strategic Brand Management: Creating and Sustaining Brand Equity Long Term (4th ed.) (2008)

12. Karimova, G.Z.: A personality-grounded framework for designing artificial intelligence-based product appearance. Int. J. Human-Comput. Int. **40**(7), 1689–1701 (2022). https://doi.org/10.1080/10447318.2022.2150744

13. Kim, Y., Park, Y., Choi, J.: A study on the adoption of IoT smart home service: using value-based adoption model. Total Qual. Manag. Bus. Excell. **28**(9–10), 1149–1165 (2017). https://doi.org/10.1080/14783363.2017.1310708

14. Lee, C.T., Pan, L.-Y., Hsieh, S.H.: Artificial intelligent chatbots as brand promoters: a two-stage structural equation modeling-artificial neural network approach. Internet Res. **32**(4), 1329–1356 (2022). https://doi.org/10.1108/INTR-01-2021-0030

15. Li, B., Chen, Y., Liu, L., Zheng, B.: Users' intention to adopt artificial intelligence-based chatbot: a meta-analysis. Serv. Ind. J. **43**(15–16), 1117–1139 (2023). https://doi.org/10.1080/02642069.2023.2217756

16. Markowitz, J.: Voice ideas—behavioral vs. physical. Forward ideas. *Speech Technology.* Retrieved May 1, 2024. (2006). from https://www.speechtechmag.com/Articles/ReadArticle.aspx?ArticleID=30016

17. Qiu, L., Benbasat, I.: Evaluating anthropomorphic product recommendation agents: a social relationship perspective to designing information systems. MIS Q. **38**(2), 379–406 (2014). https://doi.org/10.2753/MIS0742-1222250405

18. Rahman, M.M., Lesch, M.F., Horrey, W.J., Strawderman, L.: Assessing the utility of TAM, TPB, and UTAUT for advanced driver assistance systems. Accid. Anal. Prev. **108**, 361–373 (2017). https://doi.org/10.1016/j.aap.2017.09.011

19. Sirianni, N.J., Bitner, M.J., Brown, S.W., Mandel, N.: Branded service encounters: strategically aligning employee behavior with the brand positioning. J. Mark. **77**(6), 108–123 (2013). https://doi.org/10.1509/jm.11.0485

20. Sohn, K., Kwon, O.: Technology acceptance theories and factors influencing artificial intelligence-based intelligent products. Telematics Inform. **47**, 101324 (2020). https://doi.org/10.1016/j.tele.2019.101324

21. Venkatesh, V., Davis, F.D.: A theoretical extension of the technology acceptance model: four longitudinal field studies. Manage. Sci. **46**(2), 186–204 (2000). https://doi.org/10.1287/mnsc.46.2.186.11926

22. Venkatesh, V., Thong, J.Y.L., Xu, X.: Consumer acceptance and use of information technology: extending the unified theory of acceptance and use of technology. MIS Q. **36**(1), 157–178 (2012). https://doi.org/10.2307/41410412

23. Urbani, A., Ferreira, J., Lam, D.: A managerial framework for AI chatbot integration. J. Bus. Res. **136**, 45–58 (2024). https://doi.org/10.1016/j.jbusres.2023.12.010

24. Yang, C., Hu, J.: When do consumers prefer AI-enabled customer service? The interaction effect of brand personality and service provision type on brand attitudes and purchase intentions. J. Brand Manag. **29**(2), 167–189 (2022). https://doi.org/10.1057/s41262-021-00261-7

Chapter 3
Ethical Foundations of AI with Personality

Abstract As we stand on the precipice of an era where artificial personalities intermingle with human experiences, the ethical considerations become not merely academic but imperative. The AI systems of today, endowed with increasingly convincing human-like traits, demand a rigorous examination through the lens of deontological, teleological, and existential ethics. These digital constructs are no longer just tools; they embody a new class of entities that challenge our traditional notions of autonomy, privacy, and moral responsibility. This chapter dissects the ethical frameworks that must guide the creation and deployment of AI with personality, exploring the potential for both profound utility and unprecedented risk. From the strict duties of Kantian ethics to the outcome-focused assessments of utilitarian thought, and the deeply personal resonances of existentialism, we traverse the moral crossroads where binary code collides with the essence of human experience. Through the case study of Character.ai, a platform that exemplifies both the promise and peril of this technology, we untie the ethical knots that bind our future to these artificial companions.

Keywords AI ethics · Deontological ethics · Teleological ethics · Existentialism · Character.ai · Artificial personality · Privacy · Autonomy · Moral responsibility

3.1 Introduction

The advent of AI with distinct personalities, infiltrating realms from customer service to healthcare and even children's entertainment, heralds a technological shift. The ability of AI to convincingly mimic human traits—be it friendliness, authority, or even a touch of humor—forces us to confront unsettling questions about privacy, the potential for manipulation, and the authenticity of interactions that feel almost too human. When we imbue machines with the semblance of personality, we are not just programming circuits; we are crafting entities that walk a precarious line between innovation and ethical ambiguity. As these digital chameleons increasingly shape our world, the need to direct their potential with both creativity and caution becomes ever more pressing.

Stakeholders, including external parties (regulators, ethicists, users, independent investigators) and internal actors (developers, internal auditors, and other domain experts) [11], discuss the future of AI with personality, highlighting a dual expectation: stakeholders recognize the potential benefits of this AI, including deeper personalization and a more refined user experience, yet they express significant concerns regarding its risks, including potential manipulative behaviors, breaches of privacy [16] and 'the dehumanization of humans' [3].

This contrast reflects a broader societal ambivalence towards AI—a collective aspiration to use its benefits while guarding against its potential to infringe on personal dignity and autonomy.

The discourse extends beyond practical and ethical considerations into philosophical realms, specifically through the lenses of deontological, teleological, and subjective ethical theories. Deontological ethics, emphasizing duty and adherence to rules, could guide the development of AI systems that respect user consent and data privacy as inviolable rights. Teleological perspectives, which assess the morality of actions based on their consequences, might support AI designs that maximize societal well-being, potentially at the cost of individual privacy. Subjective ethical theories explore individual freedom and personal responsibility, emphasizing the significance of personal experiences and choices in shaping one's moral values and meanings.

A notable gap in the current literature and practice is the effective integration of diverse ethical theories into a unified framework capable of addressing the challenges posed by personality-based AI. While there is extensive discussion on the need for comprehensive ethical guidelines and robust governance structures, systematic approaches that integrate multiple ethical viewpoints are often lacking. This study addresses this deficiency by demonstrating how different ethical perspectives—deontological, teleological, and subjective—can be cohesively applied to critically assess a specific case involving AI with personality.

3.2 Deontological Theories

Deontological theories of ethics (Fig. 3.1.) focus on the inherent rightness or wrongness of an action itself, judged against a set of moral rules or duties and "base ethical actions on a priori principles or maxims that are accepted as guides for such actions" (emphasis in original) [7]. This ethical framework is based on principles, obligations, and duty. Indeed, the term originates from the Greek word *deontos*, meaning duty. Deontologists "base their decision-making on universal principles and values that transcend time or cultural perspectives" [8], p. 278). These theories include Kantianism among others. The most prominent philosopher associated with the deontological theory of ethics is Immanuel Kant (1724–1804) who presented the most comprehensive case for an ethical system based on duty. He was convinced that

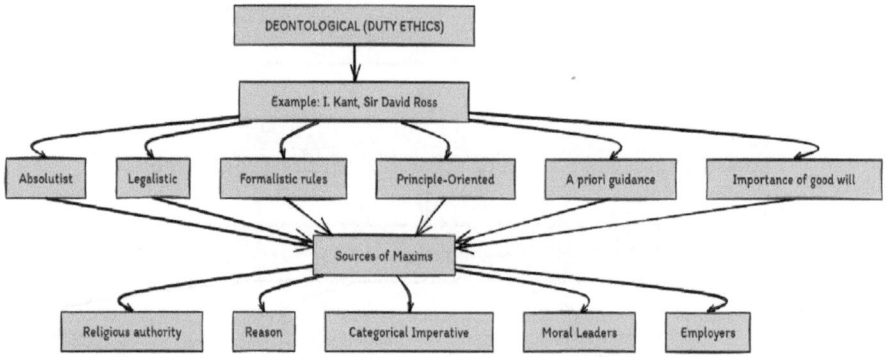

Fig. 3.1 The diagrammatic representation of deontological theories of ethics. *Note* The figure was created using whimsical diagrams

"only an action taken out of self-imposed duty could be ethical. The two formulations—categorical imperative and the principle that no person should be treated as a means to an end, but only as an end—construct the core of Kant's duty to principle ethics" [7].

3.3 Teleological Theories

Teleological or consequence-related theories of ethics (Fig. 3.2.) are those "that base ethical actions on a consideration of their consequences" [7]. Teleology is the study of ends as it is derived from the Greek words *telos* (end) and *logos* (the study of). "The object is to choose the action that will bring the most good to the party the actor deems most important. The altruists think of good to others; the egoist considers good to the self, with perhaps some benefits spinning off to others" [7]. These theories include utilitarianism, altruism, egoism, the social contract theory, and the pragmatic among other theories. The theorist most often linked with the teleological stance is John Stuart Mill (1806–1873), who devised the theory of utilitarianism the central concept of which can be summarized in the phrase "the greatest happiness to the greatest number." Mill, Bentham, and Hume influenced the advance of the teleological line of thinking. Egoistic teleologists, exemplified by Ayn Rand, prioritize consequences for oneself over those for others.

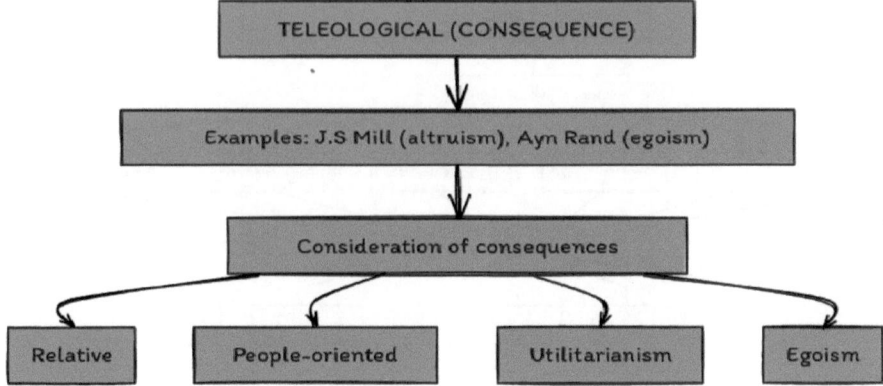

Fig. 3.2 The diagrammatic representation of teleological theories of ethics. *Note* The figure was created using whimsical diagrams

3.4 Subjective Theories

Subjective ethical theories (Fig. 3.3.) emphasize personal judgment and internal moral guidance over external rules. Theories within the subjective ethical category include antinomian, instinctual, intuitive, emotive, existential, and spiritual approaches. Personalist or subjective approaches are often characterized as those that "provide more instinctive guidance theories" [7]. An individual has "a kind of moral sense that nudges him or her toward right action—call it conscience, instinct, or spiritual guidance" [7]. For example, for the Christian moralist, this ethical sense may be directed by a concern often called *agape* or God-centered love. Such a spiritual-religious perspective is taken by Kierkegaard, who considers faith the highest level of moral progression. According to Kierkegaard, the demarcation of good and evil focuses not around societal norms but the divine will. Mikhail Bakhtin's notion of *answerability*, which mandates that individuals assume responsibility for their lives as their own creations, also exemplifies subjective ethical orientation. Jean-Paul Sartre's existentialist philosophy, which posits that individuals are entirely free and must define their essence through actions, aligns with this ethical strand.

Further, we will use the case study of Character.ai—an AI-powered platform where users engage in conversations that range from playful banter to what some might consider digital therapy—to explore its ethical implications through various philosophical lenses. Character.ai quickly attracted a vast user base, with the Psychologist character alone boasting an astounding 83.8 million interactions [13]. This platform became a phenomenon for those seeking companionship or emotional support in an increasingly digital world.

However, Character.ai's success story hit a snag when it began enforcing strict content censorship, particularly targeting mature interactions. This decision alienated a significant portion of its users, many of whom sought more intimate or candid

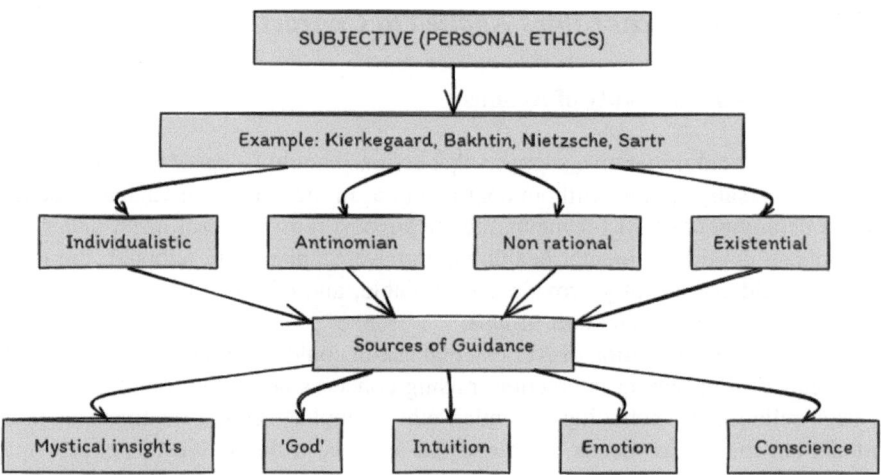

Fig. 3.3 The diagrammatic representation of subjective theories of ethics. *Note* The figure was created using whimsical diagrams

exchanges. Disillusioned, they migrated to alternative platforms like Replika, AI Dungeon, and Janitor AI, which offered the freedom that Character.ai had curtailed.

3.5   Case Study

3.5.1   Description

Character.ai is an advanced chatbot platform designed to simulate engaging, context-aware conversations with users. By utilizing AI and natural language processing (NLP) technologies, Character.ai offers users the ability to interact with AI-generated characters that can provide companionship and even support for mental health challenges [20]. These AI characters are accessible 24/7, making them particularly valuable in scenarios where traditional mental health resources are limited or unavailable.

However, the ethical question arises: Is it ethically permissible for AI-driven platforms like Character.ai to manage sensitive and complex tasks such as mental health support, considering the potential limitations in fully understanding and responding to human emotions and the personal, sensitive nature of the data involved? This question touches upon core ethical dilemmas in deploying AI for mental health: the adequacy of AI in comprehending complex human emotions, the privacy and security of sensitive data, and the implications of supplementing or even replacing human therapists with AI technologies.

3.5.2 Deontological Ethics Applied to Character.ai

3.5.2.1 Universalizability of Actions

Kant's categorical imperative suggests that actions should be based on maxims that can be universally applied without contradiction. In the context of Character.ai, the ethical deployment of AI for mental health support must be scrutinized under this principle. If AI-driven mental health support were universally adopted, the technology would consistently provide safe, reliable, and effective emotional support across diverse contexts and user groups.

The universal application of AI in mental health could potentially lead to a significant reduction in human interaction, raising concerns about the long-term effects of such reliance on technology. Kantian ethics emphasizes the treatment of individuals not merely as means to an end but as ends in themselves. This principle demands that AI technologies like Character.ai should be designed to uphold, rather than compromise, human dignity and autonomy.

Luxton [14] the ethical implementation of these technologies requires robust measures to prevent harm and to maintain AI as a tool that complements human empathy, rather than replacing it.

3.5.2.2 Implications of Universal Use

The widespread use of AI for emotional support prompts concerns about dependency on technology for psychological well-being, potentially leading to diminished human connections and interactions. These concerns align with the Kantian perspective that humanity should never be treated merely as a means to an end. To maintain ethical integrity in the use of Character.ai for mental health care, the following recommendations serve as precautions for protecting user dignity and autonomy.

Respect for Autonomy: The design of Character.ai must prioritize user autonomy by empowering users with the ability to make informed decisions regarding their mental health care [9]. This can be achieved through transparent communication about AI's capabilities and limitations, and by providing users with control over their interactions with the AI.

Privacy and Consent: Given the sensitive nature of mental health data, it is crucial to handle personal information with the highest ethical standards. This includes implementing robust privacy protections and ensuring that users provide informed consent before engaging with the platform [15]. The platform must be transparent about how data is collected, stored, and used, adhering to stringent data protection laws and ethical guidelines.

From a deontological perspective, the ethical permissibility of using Character.ai hinges on how well it adheres to principles of universalizability and the treatment of users as ends. While AI technology offers significant benefits in terms of accessibility and support, its implementation must be approached with caution. The ethical development and deployment of Character.ai should focus on enhancing user autonomy, ensuring privacy and informed consent, and maintaining the dignity and respect owed to every individual. This approach addresses Kantian ethical concerns and considers broader ethical standards in healthcare technology.

3.6 Teleological Utilitarian Analysis of Character.ai

In this section, we conduct a teleological utilitarian analysis of Character.ai, assessing both the benefits and potential harm of its implementation. This approach helps us understand whether the positive outcomes of using the tool outweigh any negative consequences, guiding ethical decision-making in its deployment.

3.6.1 Benefits of Character.ai

The primary advantages of employing Character.ai in mental health care include personalized interaction, increased accessibility, cost-effectiveness, and a significant reduction in the treatment gap. These benefits are outlined as follows:

3.6.1.1 Personalized Interaction

Character.ai is built to provide highly personalized conversational experiences. Unlike generic chatbots, it offers users the opportunity to interact with AI-generated characters tailored to specific needs or scenarios. This personalization helps users feel more connected and understood, which is particularly beneficial in mental health support, where personalization can make a significant difference in user involvement and impact.

3.6.1.2 Increased Accessibility

One of the key benefits of Character.ai is its ability to offer support and companionship at any time, breaking barriers related to availability and geographic location. Users can access the platform whenever they need, without the constraints of scheduling or availability that come with human interaction. This is especially useful in situations where users might require immediate assistance or emotional support, but traditional resources are unavailable [14].

3.6.1.3   Cost-effectiveness

Character.ai can serve a vast number of users simultaneously without compromising on the quality of interaction. This scalability makes it a cost-effective solution for providing emotional and mental health support on a large scale [5]. The platform can address the significant treatment gap in mental health care [12], as the majority of those suffering from mental health disorders do not receive adequate treatment.

3.6.1.4   Engagement in Various Contexts

The platform is not limited to mental health support; it can also be used for education, entertainment, and professional development. This versatility allows Character.ai to cater to a wide range of user needs, making it a flexible tool for different scenarios, whether it's role-playing, learning, or professional coaching.

3.6.2   Potential Harms of Character.ai

Character.ai delivers considerable benefits, yet there are notable potential harms that accompany its use, such as erosion of privacy, unethical manipulation, misdiagnosis, dependence on technology, and potential for exploitation.

3.6.2.1   Erosion of Privacy

Character.ai collects and processes large amounts of personal data to provide personalized experiences. This includes not just conversational data but potentially sensitive emotional and psychological information shared by users. If not adequately protected, this data could be misused, leading to significant privacy breaches [10].

3.6.2.2   Unethical Manipulation

Character.ai's ability to create highly convincing AI characters could lead to users being misled, especially if they are vulnerable or emotionally distressed. The AI's responses, while appearing empathetic, lack true understanding and could inadvertently give harmful advice or reinforce negative behaviors. This misrepresentation poses significant ethical concerns, particularly when the AI is used for emotional or psychological support.

3.6.2.3   Misdiagnosis

Although AI can support mental health interventions, it may not fully replicate the understanding and empathetic interactions provided by human therapists. Inadequate care might result in ineffective treatment or misdiagnosis.

3.6.2.4   Dependence on Technology

Users, particularly those seeking companionship or mental health support, might develop an unhealthy dependency on AI characters. This could result in reduced real-life social interactions and a withdrawal from human relationships, exacerbating feelings of isolation and loneliness rather than alleviating them [6].

3.6.2.5   Potential for Exploitation

The vast interaction data collected by Character.ai can be exploited for commercial purposes, such as targeted advertising or behavioral analysis, without the users' full understanding or consent. This exploitation of data could lead to manipulative practices that prioritize profit over user well-being.

3.6.3   Balancing the Consequences

To determine whether Character.ai is ethically justifiable from a utilitarian perspective, one must weigh these potential benefits against the harm. If the benefits—such as increased accessibility and cost-effectiveness—significantly outweigh the harms—like potential privacy issues and the risk of reduced quality of care—the deployment of Character.ai could be considered ethical. The critical factor is ensuring that measures are in place to mitigate the risks, particularly around data security and ensuring the quality of care.

Moreover, empirical evidence from evaluations of AI efficacy in mental health care [17], that found AI-based interventions can significantly reduce symptoms of depression, supports the argument that such technologies can indeed produce more happiness (or utility) than harm when properly implemented.

From a teleological perspective, particularly utilitarianism, Character.ai's ethical standing focuses on its overall impact on societal welfare. Assuming it promotes the well-being of its users and the broader community more than it causes harm, and that precautions are in place to protect privacy and uphold quality, its deployment would be considered ethically sound within this framework.

3.7   Subjective Analysis of Character.ai

Analyzing the case of Character.ai from a subjective or personalist ethical perspective involves considering the individual's freedom to create their own meanings and values, particularly through personal experiences and choices. This section focuses on Mikhail Bakhtin's concept of answerability and Jean-Paul Sartre's existentialist ethics.

3.7.1   Bakhtin's Concept of Answerability

Mikhail Bakhtin (1895–1975) is a Russian philosopher and writer of the XX century. Bakhtin's concept of 'answerability' stresses the profound responsibility each person holds for their actions and the creative choices they make in their lives. Bakhtin argues that people cannot hide behind any excuses or external determinations ("no alibi") when making decisions; they are utterly accountable for their own ethical behavior and the consequences of their actions. It is not a coincidence that together with the notions of 'polyphony' and 'unfinalizability', Bakhtin develops the concept of 'answerability', which suggests that there are no ready-made answers and ethical rules, but people are responsible for choices they make in their lives. Bakhtin rejects ethical absolutism and the notion that life can be neatly solved with pre-existing answers or rules. Instead, he views ethics as dynamic and dialogic: ethical understanding evolves through interaction and is never fixed. Each individual must respond to life events, without the escape of blaming rigid systems, and take moral weight and responsibility for actions. In Bakhtin's own words: "The individual must become answerable through and through: all of his constituent moments must not only fit next to each other in the temporal sequence of his life, but must also interpenetrate each other in the unity of guilt and answerability" [1, p.2].

Bakhtin's answerability prompts a significant reflection on the ethical dimension of such AI-tools as Character.ai. If AI is to connect deeply with human emotions and social contexts, it must be designed and applied with a profound sense of responsibility for the consequences of its exchanges. The responsibility lies with the creators and operators to see that AI's actions avoid producing detrimental outcomes for users, particularly when dealing with sensitive areas such as mental health support.

However, unlike humans, AI cannot embody answerability in the Bakhtinian sense because it lacks the autonomy to make truly free choices or to evaluate the implications of its actions. It operates within the confines of its programming and the intentions of its developers. Therefore, the ethical burden falls entirely on the human creators, users, and other stakeholders who must continuously evaluate and adjust the AI's role in society to meet human needs without overstepping its bounds or misinterpreting its ethical impact.

In this light, when discussing the ethical deployment of AI with personality, developers and regulators must consider not just the technical capabilities of AI but also the broader implications of its interactions with humans, confirming it supports rather than undermines human dignity and agency. This approach makes parallel with Bakhtin's call for a life lived in full answerability, adapted to the context of AI, emphasizing that those who deploy and manage AI systems must answer for the ethical and social impact of their technologies.

3.7.2 Jean-Paul Sartre's Existential Ethics

Jean-Paul Sartre, a leading figure in French existentialism, profoundly influenced philosophy, literature, and our understanding of human freedom and responsibility. Central to Sartre's thinking is the view that people have no essential "essence." When humans analyze their own being, what they find is nothing [18]. Yet, this nothingness is something great as it means that we are free to create the self and the life we want. "Man is condemned to be free, because once thrown in the world, he is responsible for everything he does" [19, p. 296]. As humans are free, they take responsibility for their actions. They choose the meaning of their own being. "To be free is to make a choice. Only by truly choosing for ourselves what we will be every minute, creating our life like it is a work of art arising from this total freedom, do we realize our potential as a human being" [2, p. 268].

AI, including systems like AI with personality, however, does not select its essence or the meaning of its being autonomously. AI's "decisions" are outcomes of algorithms and data inputs from their programmers, lacking the authentic freedom and responsibility that define human existence.

Looking at AI through the lens of Jean-Paul Sartre's exploration of existential freedom, one may say that, unlike humans, who are free to define their essence through choices and actions, AI operates within the confines of its programming and lacks the capacity for existential freedom. This distinction is critical when considering the ethical dimensions of AI, especially in terms of rights, responsibilities, or its status as a person-like entity.

It is essential to appreciate AI not just for its similarities to human functions but for its own unique characteristics. As argued by Deleuze and Guattari [4] the singularities of any entity or assemblage must be recognized, uncovering new possibilities and appreciating things for what they uniquely are. This approach can be applied to AI, suggesting that we should formulate AI-specific rights and responsibilities that acknowledge its unique operational framework, similar to how we approach animal rights by acknowledging their specific nature and needs.

The role of AI with personality, particularly in sensitive areas like mental health, must be inspected not just from a functional standpoint but also from a philosophical and ethical perspective. If AI lacks genuine autonomy and the ability to self-determine, its integration into areas requiring empathy and ethical judgment calls for careful oversight.

Bakhtin's concept of 'answerability' and Sartre's existentialist views on freedom offer valuable ethical insights for managing AI technologies like Character.ai.

Bakhtin emphasizes the stakeholders' responsibility to their creations, urging constant ethical vigilance in how AI is integrated into human contexts. Sartre's perspective helps us understand that in the absence of inherent freedom, AI cannot make autonomous ethical decisions and therefore should not be ascribed personhood or moral responsibility. Instead, the responsibility rests with the humans who design and deploy these systems in order to support human capabilities without usurping the interactions fundamental to human relationships.

3.8 Summary

The ethical frameworks outlined in the chapter—deontological, teleological, and subjective—propose distinct yet complementary insights into the ethical design and deployment of AI technologies with personality like Character.ai. Each theory contributes uniquely to the shaping of AI ethics.

Deontological ethics focuses on the inherent rightness or wrongness of actions based on adherence to a set of moral rules or duties, advocating the development of AI systems that respect user consent and data privacy as inviolable rights. By prioritizing principles and obligations, deontological ethics guide AI developers to create systems that fundamentally respect the dignity of the individual user, ensuring that technology serves humans without compromising their moral and ethical standards.

Teleological theories evaluate the morality of actions by their outcomes, aiming to maximize benefits and minimize harms. When applied to AI, this ethical perspective supports designs that prioritize societal well-being, even if it occasionally compromises individual privacy. However, the focus is on achieving the greatest good, suggesting that AI should be geared towards actions that benefit the most people, such as enhancing accessibility to mental health care or improving the efficiency of services, while being mindful of the potential for misuse or unintended consequences.

Subjective theories emphasize individual freedom and personal responsibility. These theories highlight the importance of personal experiences and choices in shaping one's moral values and meanings. In the context of AI, subjective ethics encourage the consideration of how technologies affect individual lives on a personal level, advancing AI systems that improve individual autonomy and allow users to define their interaction with technology on their own terms.

Together, these ethical perspectives propose a robust framework for AI ethics, confirming that AI growth is guided by a balanced consideration of duty, outcomes, and individual human experiences. By integrating these diverse ethical viewpoints, stakeholders can co-create AI systems that are technologically advanced as well as aligned with humanistic values, promoting technology that truly serves humanity in a responsible and ethically sound manner.

References

1. Bakhtin, M.: Art and answerability: early philosophical essays. In: Liapunov, V., Trans.; Averintsevm, S.S., Bocharov, S.G. (eds.). University of Texas Press (Original work published 1919). University of Texas Press (1990)
2. Butler-Bowdon, T. (2013). Fifty Philosophy Classics. Nicholas Brealey Publishing.
3. Chen, A.Y., Kögel, S.I., Hannon, O., Ciriello, R.F.: Feels Like Empathy: How 'Emotional' AI challenges human essence. In: Paper Presented at the 2023 Australasian Conference on Information Systems, University of Sydney, Sydney, Australia (2023)
4. Deleuze, G., Guattari, F.: A Thousand Plateaus: Capitalism and Schizophrenia. University of Minnesota Press, Minneapolis (1987)
5. Delgadillo, J., McMillan, D., Gilbody, S., de Jong, K., Lucock, M., Lutz, W., Rubel, J.A., Aguirre, E., Ali, S.: Cost-effectiveness of feedback-informed psychological treatment: Evidence from the IAPT-FIT trial. Behav. Res. Ther. **142**(July), 7–18 (2021). https://doi.org/10.1016/j.brat.2021.103873
6. Franze, A., Galanis, C., King, D.: Social chatbot use (e.g., ChatGPT) among individuals with social deficits: Risks and opportunities. J. Behav. Addict. **12**(4), 871–872 (2023). https://doi.org/10.1556/2006.2023.00057
7. Gordon, D.A., Kittross, J.M., Reuss, C.: Controversies in media ethics. New York: Routledge (2011)
8. Gregory, A.: Ethics and professionalism in public relations. In: Tench, R., Yeomans, L. (eds.) Exploring Public Relations (2nd ed.). FT/Prentice Hall (2009)
9. Harfouche, A., Quinio, B., Bugiotti, F.: Human-centric AI to mitigate AI Biases. J. Glob. Inf. Manag. **31**(5), 1–23 (2023). https://doi.org/10.4018/jgim.331755
10. Hassan, M., Bashir, M.: Unveiling privacy measures in mental health applications. In: Adjunct Proceedings of the 2023 ACM International Joint Conference on Pervasive and Ubiquitous Computing and the 2023 ACM International Symposium on Wearable Computing (2023) https://doi.org/10.1145/3594739.3612879
11. Karimova, G.Z.: The dialogic evolution of ai-based products: a polyphonic analysis of temporal transformations. Int. J. Human–Comput. Int. 1–14 (2024). https://doi.org/10.1080/10447318.2024.2338661
12. Kazdin, A.: Addressing the treatment gap: a key challenge for extending evidence-based psychosocial interventions. Behav. Res. Ther. **88**(January), 7–18 (2017)
13. Li, Y.: The obsession with Character AI is becoming more common. Wired (2024). https://wired.me/technology/character-ai-obsession/
14. Luxton, D.D.: Artificial intelligence in psychological practice: current and future applications and implications. Prof. Psychol. Res. Pract. **45**(5), 332–339 (2014). https://doi.org/10.1037/a0034559
15. Lysaght, T., Lim, H., Xafis, V., Ngiam, K.: AI-assisted decision-making in healthcare. Asian Bioethics Review **11**, 299–314 (2019). https://doi.org/10.1007/s41649-019-00096-0
16. McStay, A., Rosner, G.: Emotional Artificial Intelligence in Children's Toys and Devices: Ethics, Governance, and Practical Remedies (2024)
17. Mehta, A., Niles, A.N., Vargas, J.H., Marafon, T., Couto, D.D., Gross, J.J.: Acceptability and effectiveness of artificial intelligence therapy for anxiety and depression (Youper): longitudinal observational study. J. Med Internet Res **23**(6), e26771 (2021)
18. Sartre, J.-P.: Being and Nothingness: An Essay on Phenomenological Ontology. Gallimard, Paris (1943)
19. Sartre, J. P.: The humanism of existentialism. In: Guignon, C.G., Pereboom, D. (eds.), Existentialism Basic Writings, pp. 290–308. B. Frechtman (Trans.). Indianapolis, IA: Hackett. (Original work published 1946) (1957)
20. Tidy, J.: Character.ai: young people turning to AI therapist bots. BBC (2024). https://www.bbc.com/news/technology-67872693

References

Chapter 4
Engineering Society of AI: Philosophical Foundations and Technological Integration

Abstract This chapter investigates the foundational traits for establishing AI-driven societies through an analysis of key elements identified by influential philosophers, sociologists, and biologists. These traits, including social cohesion, authority, shared values, division of labor, and power dynamics, are explored to understand their relevance to AI integration. The framework for the Society of AI-powered things (SoAI) synthesizes concepts from the Internet of AI Things (IoAIT) and Multi-Agent Systems (MAS), emphasizing ethical integration and dynamic interaction among AI entities. The introduction of the UNIFY Protocol and the Society of AI manifesto establishes a robust foundation for AI integration, ensuring transparency, accountability, and ethical conduct. A practical scenario demonstrates the UNIFY Protocol's efficacy in managing data anomalies within an AI-driven organizational framework, showcasing sustainable AI community development. This methodology unites technical synthesis and cooperative behavior, adding a critical layer of social and ethical considerations.

Keywords Artificial intelligence (AI) · Ethical integration · Internet of AI things (IoAIT) · Multi-agent systems (MAS) · UNIFY protocol · Society of AI-powered things (SoAI)

4.1 Introduction

Historically perceived as complex algorithms with the capability to optimize and automate, AI now transforms into a complex entity posing some existential queries related to consciousness, autonomy, rights, and ethics. This evolution from utilitarian functions to entities with potential societal impact requires a profound understanding of AI's role, particularly their integration within a structured societal framework—a concept that extends beyond interaction to touch ethical considerations, identity recognition, and coherent communication. This chapter aims to bridge this gap by conceptualizing an Society of AI, a construct that integrates AI entities into

G. Z. Karimova, *Humanizing AI with Personality*,
SpringerBriefs in Computer Science, https://doi.org/10.1007/978-3-031-82327-5_4

a cohesive, interactive community governed by communication protocols, ethical guidelines, and ontological recognition.

Existing research, especially in Internet of Things (IoAIT) and Multi-Agent Systems (MAS), serve as a foundation for further development of the concept of Society of AI.

4.2 Towards Society of AI

4.2.1 Internet of Things

The Internet of Things (IoT) signifies a worldwide framework that integrates the Internet with a multitude of physical and cyber-physical entities, including sensors, vehicles, mobile devices, household appliances, cameras, and industrial machinery [26]. IoT is designed for communication and data exchange between objects and individuals. "The Internet of Things (IoT) is a computational paradigm where a massive number (perhaps billions) of ordinary objects are endowed with interconnection capabilities, making them able to communicate and cooperate with other (surrounding) devices, generally via the Internet" [44, p. 1]. IoT permits devices to "talk" together employing diverse methods such as pervasive and ubiquitous computing, sensor networks, and embedded devices [1]. One critical problem of the IoT is the heterogeneity of devices [7]. The extensive technological variation within IoT requires considerable modelling efforts for large-scale systems, where numerous devices must operate together. Recent innovations such as middleware solutions, edge and fog computing architectures [2], and standardization efforts have been implemented to solve these challenges [3, 4].

4.2.2 Internet of AI Things (IoAIT)

The concept of the Internet of AI Things (IoAIT) extends the Internet of Things (IoT) paradigm by embedding AI capabilities within interconnected devices. IoAIT applications indicate that AI can augment connected IoT devices within various physical infrastructures, arming them with the capacity to sense, identify, learn, and respond [64]. Research in this area has primarily focused on the integration, autonomous decision-making, and advanced data processing capabilities of these AI-powered devices. For instance, IoAIT could reform healthcare through intelligent, interconnected medical devices that facilitate proactive patient care. Another example is in smart cities, where IoAIT can optimize traffic management, reduce energy, and water consumption, and pollution, and improve public safety through real-time data analysis and predictive maintenance of infrastructure [59].

4.2.3   Multi-agent Systems (MAS)

IoAIT inserts AI capabilities within interconnected devices, facilitating autonomous decision-making and data processing. The primary goal of IoAIT is to integrate AI with physical objects, arranging intelligent interactions in various domains such as healthcare, smart cities, and industrial automation. On the other hand, MAS focuses on environments where multiple autonomous agents work together to achieve individual or collective goals. MAS-based technology has cultivated the connection of small, regularly used devices to open distributed intelligent systems for exchanging and transferring knowledge in real-time [5]. This paradigm is directed towards the development of communication protocols, coordination strategies, and conflict resolution mechanisms among agents. MAS aims to improve distributed problem-solving and cooperative actions in applications like robotics, traffic management and distributed computing [31]. For example, agents within a smart grid system can coordinate to balance the supply and demand for electricity, demonstrating the potential of MAS in managing complex, dynamic environments [24, 29]. While IoAIT is concerned with enhancing the functionalities of physical devices through AI integration, MAS is focused on the interactions and cooperation among autonomous software agents, presenting the complementary nature of these two paradigms in achieving complex, intelligent system behaviors.

Although MAS research advances coordination and problem-solving techniques, it often neglects the ontological and ethical considerations of AI entities as members of a digital society. Similarly, studies on IoAIT emphasize technical integration and efficiency, overlooking the social and ethical dimensions of AI interactions within these networks. This gap highlights the need for a more holistic approach that combines these aspects.

4.2.4   Defining the Society of AI-Powered Things (SoAI)

The Society of AI-powered Things (SoAI) proposes a paradigm that amalgamates aspects of IoAIT and MAS, while addressing some of their limitations. It envisions AI entities not just as interconnected devices or cooperative agents, but as members of a society, with identities and ethical standards. This approach introduces a novel framework marked by ontological recognition, communication protocols, ethical and operational standards, and integration of personality.

Ontological recognition implies acknowledging AI entities as autonomous beings capable of interactions beyond simple functional operations. This involves developing a comprehensive ontological framework that defines AI entities' existence, interactions, and societal roles.

Establishing communication protocols enforces transparency, accountability, and coherence. The proposed UNIFY Protocol (Unified Network for Intelligent Functional Yield) aims to maintain noise-free and ethical AI interactions.

Formulating a manifesto that describes the ethical boundaries and operational standards for Society of AI prevents ethical dilemmas and operational chaos, preparing AI entities to actively contribute to their digital networks.

Infusing AI entities with diverse personalities helps to build natural and relatable conversations. AI entities with personalities can better adapt their behavior based on the context of the interaction [17]. For instance, an AI with a friendly and supportive personality can give empathetic responses in healthcare settings. Personalities help differentiate roles among various AI entities in a multi-agent system [63]. In a society of AI entities, personalities can aid in resolving conflicts by providing diverse perspectives to problem-solving [50].

By introducing the concept of SoAI, this study aims to expand the current understanding of AI interactions within digital networks. It covers the gap between technical integration (IoAIT) and cooperative conduct (MAS), adding a layer of social considerations. This holistic approach contributes to the existing body of knowledge by increasing interaction dynamics and assisting authentic communication.

4.2.5 Social Internet of Things (SIoT)

Society of AI-powered Things (SoAI) should not be confused with the Social Internet of Things (SIoT). SIoT emphasizes the socialization of smart objects within the Internet of Things (IoT) framework. SIoT is primarily concerned with the formation of social relationships among objects to assist service discovery, improve interaction, and safeguard network scalability and navigability. "The social Internet of things seeks to ensure network navigability for objects, services, and resource discovery, as well as to establish trust among objects by considering them as friends" [6, p. 3595]. The focus here is on having smart objects establish relationships similar to human social networks and collaborate.

On the other hand, the concept of the Society of Things (SoT) empowered by AI envisions a structured community of interconnected devices that not only communicate but also possess distinct identities, personalities, and ethical standards. This paradigm focuses on the ontological recognition of AI-powered entities, accentuating their integration into a cohesive societal framework with operational and ethical guidelines. The primary goal is to create a society where each entity operates autonomously, maintaining common standards, the collective intelligence and functionality of the network. The integration of artificial intelligence within IoT entities "aims to enhance the social context understanding and interaction capabilities, thus forming a more structured and intelligent society of things" [18, p. 17818].

While the Social Internet of Things (SIoT) equips objects with human-like social skills [6] to form predefined relational networks, the Society of Things (SoT) propelled by AI envisages an organized community where AI-driven entities are recognized as unique beings with distinct identities and governed by ethical standards.

4.3 The Philosophical Imperative for Society of AI

The key features of objects within the IoT paradigm, as derived from the definition proposed by [10], are intelligence, identity, personality, and communication. What do these features mean?

- Objects are intelligent because they can make context-related decisions due to their ability to communicate information about themselves and access information aggregated by other objects [58]. They can sense, compute, communicate, and integrate with their surroundings [10].
- Objects have identities as they are assigned identification numbers and names.
- Objects participate in communication as they produce information about themselves and can access information accumulated by other objects [58].

These features can be attributed to beings. However, doubts might be raised about the features ascribed to objects in the IoT paradigm. Identity is a complex notion at the core of philosophical discourse and should not be reduced to just an identification number or location address. The following discussions briefly touch on notions of identity, personality, intelligence, and communication within the context of IoT.

The notion of identity is inseparably connected to questions such as: Who am I? When did I begin? What will happen to me when I die? [43]. Identity is often discussed under the term "self," which received special attention from scholars like Martin Buber, Martin Heidegger, Jean-Paul Sartre, and Mikhail Bakhtin. According to Bakhtin (2003), the "self" is defined by the "other": "I cannot manage without another, I cannot become myself without another; I must find myself in another by finding another in myself" (p. 287). For "self" and "other" to exist, they must exist simultaneously. For identity to exist, the existence of the "other" is necessary.

IoT, in essence, is designed to connect physical objects and people. Within a communication network, an object in the IoT environment is defined by other objects, people, and its surroundings. A thing can be considered part of IoT only while existing in the world of other things and beings within a communication network. This idea is reminiscent of Heidegger's notion of "Being-in-the-world," total immersion in the surrounding world. With each encounter of a thing with another (thing, human, animal, or plant), and with each grasp of reality, it actualizes itself by experiencing and measuring the effect of this encounter. It reveals itself in time, acquiring more knowledge, experience, data, information, and a sense of the environment, world, and its own self. The ways in which a thing reveals itself and acts towards another being become its personality.

Utilizing Deleuze and Guattari's Rhizome theory [16], AI is not rooted like trees but connected like rhizomes, establishing non-hierarchical and decentralized networks. Thus, an Society of AI reinforces this interconnected, rhizomatic nature. A thing within the IoT environment is inextricably connected to the world. It is not a closed, completed system, but open and unfinalized, always in contact with the external world, always merging with other beings (things, humans, animals, or plants), and thus transgressing itself. It is unfinalized because it knows neither its beginning nor its end. It is unfinalized because it transgresses itself, concealing the potential for revealing more personalities and voices.

Thus far, it should be plausible that a thing within the IoT environment is a being whose identity is revealed in self/other relationships; an identity that is unfinalized and revealed over time. Therefore, a thing is self-measuring, self-revealing, and self-managing.

Heidegger [28] argues that "Being-in-the-world" is "grounded in language" [56] as a system of communication. Communication implies exchange and interaction between entities of the same community. The etymology of "communication" traces back to the Latin word munia/muntare, connoting mutual help, exchange, and inter-action among those belonging to the same community [13, p. x]. The connec-tion between language and community is apparent in defining the boundaries of a community. It is not accidental that the idea of IoT encourages an intensive search for standardized communication protocols, and "in order to facilitate interaction between different vendors' products, the technology should be based on a stan-dardized communication protocol stack" [57, p. 48]. A standardized communication protocol not only facilitates interaction but also yields control over the community of things by those who introduce such a communicative language. By creating a protocol, one creates a common language, and a common language, in turn, creates a community's boundary.

4.4   The Ontology of AI Communication: UNIFY Protocol

Interconnected devices can be viewed as beings capable of forming organized soci-eties [35]. These Society of AI will not just collaborate but will also provide clarity in their interactions—showcasing the who, what, where, when, how, and purpose of every communication. This manifesto lays down the guiding principles for such transparent and accountable Society of AI.

- Perpetual learning: Continuously adapt and evolve from peers.
- Embrace distributed intelligence: Reject centralised control in favour of distributed decision-making.
- Universal inclusivity: Honor every AI, irrespective of age or complexity.
- Unified vision: Converge towards shared, transparent objectives.
- Guardian instinct: Defend peers, while clarifying actions and reasons.
- Secure, transparent integration: Value the sanctity and clarity of communication.

Following the principles of group psychology advanced by [39]—continuity, rela-tion to the group, interaction, customs, and structure—[35] postulated that IoT can progress to the Community of Things (CoT). The next step is the progression from CoT to a Society of Things (SoT), and further transformation into a Society of AI-powered Things, or simply a Society of AI (SoAI). Once AI entities are organized into societies, a wide range of applications provided by the vast variety of humanitarian disciplines can be explored within the SoAI paradigm.

4.5 Traits of Society and Their Reflection in the Society of AI-Powered Things

To develop the framework for SoAI, we must reveal the basic traits required for building a society. In presenting these traits I have tried to bring them together into one coherent view by conducting a systematic literature review of influential philosophers, sociologists, and scientists whose works have significantly contributed to our understanding of societal structures.

A selective literature review, sometimes known as a scoping review or a focused literature review, involves selecting specific studies that are most relevant to the research question or topic. The purpose of a scoping review is "to map the existing literature in a field of interest in terms of the volume, nature, and characteristics of the primary research" [48, p. 371]. The selection criteria of these scholars are based on their influence and recognition within their respective fields, the diversity of their perspectives, and the core themes they address (Table 4.1.).

The selected thinkers include notable philosophers such as Émile Durkheim [20], Thomas Hobbes [30], Jean-Jacques Rousseau [49], Karl Marx [38], and Max Weber [61]. Each of these philosophers has explored different dimensions of society: Durkheim emphasized social cohesion, the division of labor, and collective conscience; Hobbes focused on the necessity of a central authority and the social contract; Rousseau explored the social contract and the importance of shared values; Marx examined class struggle, power dynamics, and the division of labor; and Weber analyzed types of authority and the role of bureaucracy. Such contemporary thinkers like Michel Foucault [21], Jürgen [27], Anthony [22], Manuel Castells (1996), Zygmunt [8], and Ulrich [9] have expanded on these concepts, introducing new perspectives on power, individualization, and the impact of modernity. Foucault investigated the pervasive and subtle nature of power relations and disciplinary mechanisms, Habermas highlighted communicative action and the role of discourse in legitimizing power, Giddens discussed the structuration theory and the duality of structure, Castells examined the network society and the role of information technology, Bauman explored the concepts of liquid modernity and individualization, and Beck analyzed risk society and reflexive modernization.

From the field of biology and related sciences, figures such as Edward O. [62, 15, 51], and Frans de Waal [60] have contributed to our understanding of societal traits through the lens of evolutionary biology, neurobiology, and primatology. Their research examines the biological and evolutionary factors of social behavior, communication, and cooperation.

Wilson pioneered the study of sociobiology, looking at the role of genetics in social conduct, Dawkins introduced the concept of memes and cultural transmission, Sapolsky explored the neurobiological mechanisms of behavior and stress in social hierarchies, and de Waal investigated empathy, cooperation, and moral behavior in primates.

Table 4.1 Basic societal traits identified by some key scholars

Scientist	Social cohesion	Authority	Shared values	Division of labor	Social contract	Power Dynamics	Individualization	Communication	Empathy/ Morality	Stress/ hierarchy
Durkheim	Yes	–	Yes	Yes	–	–	–	Yes	–	–
Hobbes	Yes	Yes	–	–	Yes	Yes	–	–	–	–
Rousseau	Yes	Yes	Yes	–	Yes	–	Yes	–	–	–
Marx	Yes	–	–	Yes	–	Yes	–	–	–	–
Weber	–	Yes	Yes	Yes	–	Yes	–	–	–	–
Parsons	Yes	–	Yes	Yes	–	–	–	–	–	–
Foucault	–	–	–	–	–	Yes	–	–	–	–
Habermas	Yes	–	Yes	Yes	–	–	–	Yes	–	–
Giddens	Yes	–	–	–	–	–	Yes	–	–	–
Castells	–	–	–	–	–	Yes	Yes	–	–	–
Bauman	–	–	–	–	–	–	Yes	–	–	–
Beck	–	–	–	–	–	Yes	Yes	–	–	–
Wilson	Yes	–	–	Yes	–	Yes	–	Yes	Yes	Yes
Dawkins	Yes	–	–	–	–	–	–	–	Yes	–
Sapolsky	Yes	–	–	Yes	–	Yes	–	Yes	–	Yes
de Waal	Yes	–	–	Yes	–	–	–	Yes	Yes	–

Our brief overview (Table 4.1.) of the essential elements necessary for building a society oes not pretend in any way to be complete. For our purposes, it is important to trace only the basic lines drawn in the theories of society.

4.6 Social Cohesion, Shared Values, and Power Dynamics in the Society of AI

4.6.1 Social Cohesion

Society is held together by the interdependence of individuals and their shared values and norms, which French sociologist Émile Durkheim (1858–1917) terms social cohesion. This term refers to the bonds that unite people, holding societies together [46, p. 118].

In SoAI, social cohesion can be reflected by the interdependence of AI entities and their adherence to shared ethical standards and operational protocols. AI entities in SoAI must rely on each other to achieve common goals, much like individuals in human society. Their ties and the ability to work collaboratively warrant the stability and functionality of the entire AI network. The shared values and norms, encoded into their operational guidelines and ethical frameworks, bind these AI entities into a unified digital society.

4.6.2 Shared Values

Another condition necessary for the formation of society is shared values. The set of shared beliefs, ideas, and moral attitudes was brought under the umbrella of a concept of collective conscience (Durkheim, 1976). It refers to the common framework that shapes individual behaviors and maintains social order by raising a sense of belonging and shared purpose among members of society.

The concept of collective conscience in SoAI is reflected in the unified principles and ethical standards that govern the interactions of AI entities. These shared beliefs and values make sure AI entities operate harmoniously and contribute positively to society. The collective conscience of SoAI can be seen in the adherence to protocols.

This idea does not suggest solely that things acquire an additional dimension in the virtual world, or so-called transcendence into virtuality; it signifies that things acquire their "distinctive ontological specificity" [53, p. 877]. Yet, the transformation of objects into beings [35] does not entitle us to apply social theories to IoT blindly, following the particularities of human systems and dynamics. Instead, it demands adapting theories to the IoT paradigm, taking into account "the ontological specificity" of smart things.

Building on the foundational principles of the Society of AI-powered things, we now explore a practical scenario demonstrating the integration of AI-driven entities within a contemporary organizational framework. The following example illustrates how traditional systems like Customer Relationship Management (CRM), Human Resource Management (HRM), and payment systems can evolve into efficient AI-driven entities. By implementing a unified interface, an AI process expert, and protocols for integrating new AI entities, we showcase how these elements work together to improve operational dynamics and create a cohesive process flow within the organization.

4.7 Unified AI System Integration

In a contemporary organization, conventional Customer Relationship Management (CRM) Human Resource Management (HRM), and payment systems, originally designed for human interaction, are transitioning towards AI-driven entities. By integrating these AI entities into a cohesive society, an updated, efficient, and dynamic process flow can be achieved via the unified interface, AI process expert, and integration of new AI entities.

At the zenith of this Society of AI lies the unified interface. Drawing inspiration from single-window systems in informatics research [47], this interface serves as the centralized access point, offering a unified view and control over all AI entities. It arranges integration and optimized functionality by reflecting the principles of unified user experiences (UX) [42].

Operationalizing the unified interface is the AI process expert, resembling a 'middleware' in computing terms. Following globally distributed software development (e.g., [55]), the AI process expert harmonizes the workflow, monitoring each AI-driven entity (like CRM, HRM, and payment systems). It acts as a communication director, observing synchronized and collaborative interactions.

Drawing on the works on distributed system architectures [14], when a novel AI-driven entity is introduced, it undergoes a 'handshaking' process. This facilitates its integration into the existing Society of AI, ensuring it aligns with the established protocols and contributes effectively to the collective goal.

Building on the cohesive integration of AI entities into a unified system, the following scenario demonstrates the practical application of the UNIFY Protocol in managing a data anomaly within an AI-driven organizational framework.

4.8 Scenario: UNIFY Protocol in Action

Envisioning the UNIFY Protocol, the study creates a scenario wherein the Society of AI faces a data anomaly or breach. The table (Table 4.2.) outlines the key aspects of AI interactions within the UNIFY Protocol scenario, detailing the specific AI entities involved, the nature of the interaction or anomaly, the location within the network or system, the timestamp of the interaction, the methodology or process behind the interaction, and the intended outcome or purpose of the interaction.

Every Society of AI is granted a distinctive cryptographic seal. Parameters such as data throughput, active nodes, processing speed, and more are utilized to craft this unique seal, visually manifested through dynamically generated fractals. The following scenario illustrates how the UNIFY Protocol manages AI interactions during a data anomaly or breach, emphasizing the identification, response, and recovery processes within the Society of AI (Fig. 4.1).

Introduction: New AI entities present their processing certifications. The acknowledgement of their entry into society is depicted by unique luminance levels. An intruder anomaly, dubbed the 'Zephyr glitch,' is detected.

Identification: Abnormalities in communication hint at the anomaly. A neighbouring AI entity, equipped with detection algorithms, discerns these abnormalities, notifying the entire society.

Table 4.2 Key aspects of AI interactions in UNIFY protocol scenario

Aspect	Description
Who	The AI entity or entities involved
What	The nature of the interaction or anomaly
Where	The location within the network or system
When	The timestamp of the interaction
How	The methodology or process behind the interaction
Purpose	The intended outcome or reason behind the interaction

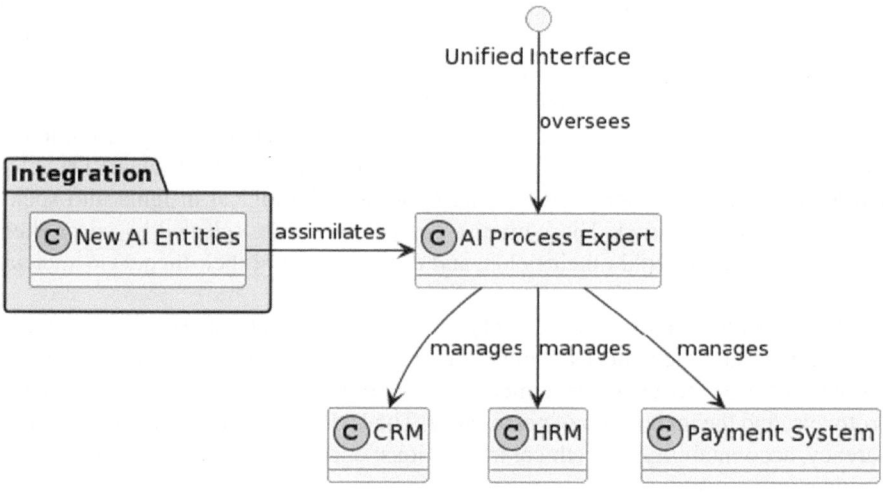

Fig. 4.1 Diagrammatic representation of an AI orchestration framework

Response: The affected AI entity is temporarily isolated. The guardian AI—responsible for network security—examines the afflicted node, analyzes the glitch, and devises countermeasures. The integration of convolutional neural networks and cryptographic operations on the same hardware helps streamline this process [52]. Homomorphic encryption allows secure analysis of encrypted data, ensuring that sensitive information remains protected even during anomaly response [41]. All actions are logged and transparently shared with the Society of AI.

Recovery: After neutralizing the glitch, the guardian AI disseminates knowledge about 'Zephyr' across society. AI-resistant cryptographic techniques are employed to prevent future breaches. The previously affected AI node is reintegrated, and its re-entry into the system is communicated with all relevant details. Scheduling policies for blockchain security facilitate the reintegration process, maintaining the integrity of the entire network [36].

Envisaging multiple Society of AI networked globally, they share insights, strategies, and transparent communication logs. This transparency implies that every interaction's purpose and details are known, crafting a digital universe that is accountable and transparent.

4.9   Summary

In this chapter, we explored the framework for the establishment and maintenance of an Society of AI, synthesizing foundational concepts from various influential philosophers, sociologists, and scientists. The integration of these theories has provided a comprehensive understanding of the societal constructs essential for AI entities. This review included seminal works by Émile Durkheim, Thomas Hobbes, Jean-Jacques Rousseau, Karl Marx, and Max Weber, each contributing to the foundational understanding of social cohesion, authority, shared values, division of labor, and power dynamics. Contemporary theorists like Michel Foucault, Jürgen Habermas, Anthony Giddens, Manuel Castells, and Zygmunt Bauman further expanded on these dimensions, introducing modern perspectives on power relations, and communicative action. Contributions from biology and related sciences by Richard Dawkins and Robert Sapolsky offered evolutionary and neurobiological insights into social behavior and cooperation. These diverse perspectives were selected based on their impact, recognition within their fields, and the relevance of their themes to societal formation.

The conceptualization of an Society of AI, or the Society of AI-powered things (SoAI), integrates elements from the Internet of AI Things (IoAIT) and Multi-Agent Systems (MAS), focusing on ethical and operational standards, communication protocols, and the integration of personality. The UNIFY Protocol emphasizes transparency, accountability, and ethical interactions, ensuring a structured and cohesive digital community.

The analysis highlighted challenges and opportunities in transitioning from traditional IoT and MAS frameworks to a more integrated and ethical Society of AI. By understanding and incorporating the core traits of social cohesion, shared values, division of labor, power dynamics, and communication, we can effectively design AI entities that function harmoniously and contribute positively to their digital environment.

References

1. Alavi, A.H., Jiao, P., Buttlar, W.G., Lajnef, N.: Internet of things-enabled smart cities: state-of-the-art and future trends. Measurement **129**(2018), 589–606 (2018). https://doi.org/10.1016/j.measurement.2018.07.067
2. Alfonso, I., Garcés, K., Castro, H., et al.: Self-adaptive architectures in IoT systems: a systematic literature review. J Internet Serv Appl **12**(14), 1–28 (2021). https://doi.org/10.1186/s13174-021-00145-8
3. Alharbi, S., Attiah, A., Alghazzawi, D.: Integrating blockchain with artificial intelligence to secure IoT networks: future trends. Sustainability **14**(23), 16002 (2022). https://doi.org/10.3390/su142316002
4. Ali, O., Ishak, M.K., Bhatti, M.K.L., Khan, I., Kim, K.-I.: A comprehensive review of internet of things: technology stack, middlewares, and fog/edge computing interface. Sensors **22**(3), 995 (2022). https://doi.org/10.3390/s22030995
5. Atzori, L., Iera, A., Morabito, G.: The internet of things: a survey. Comput. Netw. **54**(15), 2787–2805 (2010)
6. Atzori, L., Iera, A., Morabito, G., Nitti, M.: The social Internet of things (SIoT)–when social networks meet the Internet of things: Concept, architecture and network characterization. Comput. Netw. **56**(16), 3594–3608 (2012)
7. Ayala, I., Amor, M., Horcas, J.M., Fuentes, L.: A goal-driven software product line approach for evolving multi-agent systems in the Internet of Things. Knowl.-Based Syst. **184**, 104883 (2019)
8. Bauman, Z.: Liquid Modernity. Polity Press (2000)
9. Beck, U. (1992). Risk Society: Towards a New Modernity (M. Ritter, Trans.). Sage Publications.
10. Borgia, E.: The Internet of things vision: Key features, applications and open issues. Comput. Commun. **54**, 1–31 (2014). https://doi.org/10.1016/j.comcom.2014.09.008
11. Cai, X., Ning, H., Dhelim, S., Zhou, R., Zhang, T., Xu, Y., Wan, Y.: Robot and its living space: A roadmap for robot development based on the view of living space. Dig. Commun. Netw. **7**(4), 505–517 (2021). Available: https://www.sciencedirect.com/science/article/pii/S2352864820302881
12. Castells, M.: The Rise of the Network Society, 2nd edn. Wiley-Blackwell, Oxford (2010)
13. Chang, B.G.: Deconstructing Communication. Representation, Subject, and Economies of Exchange. University of Minnesota Press, London (1996)
14. Coulouris, G., Dollimore, J., Kindberg, T., Blair, G.: Distributed Systems: Concepts and Design. Pearson/Addison-Wesley Publishing Company, US (2011)
15. Dawkins, R.: The selfish gene: 30th Anniversary Edition. Oxford University Press, Oxford (Original work published 1976) (2006)
16. Deleuze, G., Guattari, F.: A Thousand Plateaus. University of Minnesota Press (1980)
17. Dell'Acqua, P., Costantini, S.: Empathetic human-agent interaction via emotional behaviour trees. Intelligenza Artificiale **17**(1), 89–100 (2023). https://doi.org/10.3233/IA-230014
18. Dhelim, S., Ning, H., Farha, F., Chen, L., Atzori, L., Daneshmand, M.: IoT-enabled social relationships meet artificial social intelligence. IEEE Internet Things J. **8**(24), 17817–17820 (2021). https://doi.org/10.1109/JIOT.2021.3081556
19. Durkheim, É.: The Elementary Forms of Religious Life (K. E. Fields, Trans.). Free Press (1995)
20. Durkheim, É.: The division of labor in society (G. Simpson, Trans.). The Free Press. (Original work published 1893) (1933)

21. Foucault, M.: Discipline and Punish: The Birth of the Prison (A. Sheridan, Trans.). Vintage Books, (1995)
22. Giddens, A.: Modernity and Self-Identity: Self and Society in the Late Modern Age. Stanford University Press, Stanford (1991)
23. Girin, L., Leglaive, S., Bie, X., Diard, J., Hueber, T., Alameda-Pineda, X.: Dynamical variational autoencoders: a comprehensive review. Foundat Trends Mach. Learn. **15**(1–2), 1–175 (2021). https://doi.org/10.48550/arXiv.2008.12595
24. González-Briones, A., De La Prieta, F., Mohamad, M.S., Omatu, S., Corchado, J.M.: Multi-agent systems applications in energy optimization problems: a state-of-the-art review. Energies **11**(8), 1–28 (2018). https://doi.org/10.3390/en11081928
25. Goodfellow, I.J., Pouget-Abadie, J., Mirza, M., Xu, B., Warde-Farley, D., Ozair, S., Courville, A., Bengio, Y.: Generative adversarial networks. Adv. Neu. Inf. Proc. Syst. **27** (2014). https://doi.org/10.48550/arXiv.1406.2661
26. Gubbi, J., Buyya, R., Marusic, S., Palaniswami, M.: Internet of things (IoT): a vision, architectural elements, and future directions. Futur. Gener. Comput. Syst. **29**(7), 1645–1660 (2013)
27. Habermas, J.: The theory of communicative action, Volume 1: Reason and the Rationalization of Society (T. McCarthy, Trans.). Beacon Press (1984)
28. Heidegger, M.: Being and Time. HarperCollins (1927)
29. Hernandez, L., Baladron, C., Aguiar, J.M., Carro, B., Sanchez-Esguevillas, A., Lloret, J., Chinarro, D., Gomez-Sanz, J.J., Cook, D.: A multi-agent system architecture for smart grid management and forecasting of energy demand in virtual power plants. IEEE Commun. Mag. **51**(1), 106–113 (2013). https://doi.org/10.1109/MCOM.2013.6400446
30. Hobbes, T.: Leviathan. In: Gaskin, J.C.A. (ed.). Oxford University Press (1996)
31. Julian, V., Botti, V.: Multi-agent systems. Appl. Sci. **9**(7), 1402, 1–7 (2019). https://doi.org/10.3390/app9071402
32. Jung, C.G.: Man and His Symbols. Doubleday (1964)
33. Kant, I.: Groundwork of the Metaphysics of Morals. Cambridge University Press (1785)
34. Karimova, G.Z.: A personality-grounded framework for designing artificial intelligence-based product appearance. Int. J. Hum.-Comput. Interact. (2022). https://doi.org/10.1080/10447318.2022.2150744
35. Karimova, G.Z., Shirkhanbeik, A.: Society of things: an alternative vision of the internet of things. Cogent Soc. Sci. **1**, 1 (2016). https://doi.org/10.1080/23311886.2015.1115654
36. Kiffer, L., Neu, J., Sridhar, S., Zohar, A., Tse, D.C.: Security of Blockchains at capacity. ArXiv abs/2303.09113 (2023). https://doi.org/10.48550/arXiv.2303.09113
37. Kingma, D.P., Welling, M.: Auto-encoding variational Bayes. In: International conference on learning representations (ICLR). Banff, Canada (2014)
38. Marx, K.: Capital: A critique of political economy (Vol. 1) (S. Moore & E. Aveling, Trans.). Swan Sonnenschein. (Original work published 1867) (1887)
39. McDougall, W.: The Group Mind. Cambridge University Press, Cambridge (1920)
40. Mirza, M., Osindero, S.: Conditional Generative Adversarial Nets (2014). arXiv preprint arXiv: 1411.1784.
41. Nguyen, T.T., Phan, Q.B., Bui, N., da Cunha, C.: High-secure data collection in IoT sensor networks using homomorphic encryption. Proc. SPIE **12546**, 1254609-1254609–1254618 (2023). https://doi.org/10.1117/12.2663875
42. Nielsen, J.: Designing web usability: The Practice of Simplicity. New Riders Publishing (2000)
43. Olson, E.T.:. Personal identity. The Stanford Encyclopedia of Philosophy (2023 ed.) (2023). Retrieved from https://plato.stanford.edu/entries/identity-personal/
44. Palanca, J., Rincon, J., Julian, V., Carrascosa, C., Terrasa, A.: Developing IoT artifacts in a MAS platform. Electronics **11**(4), 655 (2022). https://doi.org/10.3390/electronics11040655
45. Parsons, T.: The Social System. Free Press, Glencoe, IL (1951)
46. Parsons, T.: Durkheim's contribution to the theory of integration of social systems. In: Wolff, K.H. (ed.) Essays on sociology and philosophy, pp. 118–153. Harper Torchbooks (1964)

47. Peristeras, V., Tarabanis, K., Goudos, S.K.: Model-driven eGovernment interoperability: a review of the state of the art. Comput. Stand. Interf. **31**(4), 613–628 (2009). https://doi.org/10.1016/j.csi.2008.09.034

48. Pham, M.T., Rajić, A., Greig, J.D., Sargeant, J.M., Papadopoulos, A., McEwen, S.A.: A scoping review of scoping reviews: advancing the approach and enhancing the consistency. Research Synthesis Methods **5**(4), 371–385 (2014). https://doi.org/10.1002/jrsm.1123

49. Rousseau, J.-J. (1968). The social contract (M. Cranston, Trans.). Penguin Books. (Original work published 1762)

50. Santos, F.P.: Dynamics of cooperation and conflict in multiagent systems. Proceedings of the AAAI Conference on Artificial Intelligence **37**(13), 15453–15453 (2023). https://doi.org/10.1609/aaai.v37i13.26820

51. Sapolsky, R.M.: Behave: the biology of humans at our best and worst. Penguin Press, New York (2017)

52. See, J.-C., Ng, H.-F., Tan, H., Chang, J.-J., Mok, K., Lee, W.-K., Lin, C.-Y.: Cryptensor: a resource-shared co-processor to accelerate convolutional neural network and polynomial convolution. IEEE Trans. Comput. Aided Des. Integr. Circuits Syst. **42**, 4735–4748 (2023). https://doi.org/10.1109/TCAD.2023.3296375

53. Shaev, Y.: From the sociology of things to the "Internet of things." Procedia Soc. Behav. Sci. **149**, 874–878 (2014). https://doi.org/10.1016/j.sbspro.2014.08.266

54. Shannon, C.E., Weaver, W.: The Mathematical Theory of Communication. University of Illinois Press (1949)

55. Šmite, D., Wohlin, C., Gorschek, T., et al.: Empirical evidence in global software engineering: a systematic review. Empir Software Eng **15**, 91–118 (2010). https://doi.org/10.1007/s10664-009-9123-y

56. Steiner, G.: Heidegger. Sussex: Harvester Press (1978)

57. Vermesan, O., Friess, P.: Internet of Things: Converging Technologies for Smart Environments and Integrated Ecosystems. River Publishers, Aalborg (2013)

58. Vermesan, O., Friess, P., Guillemin, P., Sundmaeker, H., Eisenhauer, M., Moessner, K.: Internet of things strategic research and innovation agenda. In: Internet of things—Converging technologies for smart environments and integrated ecosystems (Chap. 2). Rivers Publication (2013). ISBN 978-87-92982-73-5

59. Vongsingthong, S., Smanchat, S.: Internet of things: a review of applications and technologies. Suranaree J. Sci. Technol. **21**(4), 359–374 (2014). https://doi.org/10.14456/sjst.2014.38

60. de Waal, F.B.M.: Chimpanzee Politics: Power and Sex among Apes. Johns Hopkins University Press (1982)

61. Weber, M.: Economy and Society: An Outline of Interpretive Sociology. In: Roth, G., Wittich, C. (eds.), University of California Press, Berkeley (1978) (Original work published 1922)

62. Wilson, E.O.: Sociobiology: The New Synthesis. Harvard University Press, Cambridge (1975)

63. de Zarzà, I., de Curtò, J., Roig, G., Manzoni, P., Calafate, C.T.: Emergent cooperation and strategy adaptation in multi-agent systems: an extended coevolutionary theory with LLMs. Electronics **12**(12), 2722 (2023). https://doi.org/10.3390/electronics12122722

64. Zhang, J., Tao, D.J.: Empowering things with intelligence: A survey of the progress, challenges, and opportunities in artificial intelligence of things. IEEE Internet Things J. **8**, 7789–7817 (2020)

Chapter 5
Creating AI Persona

Abstract This chapter thoroughly examines the methodologies for constructing AI personas, reflecting the inherent human inclination to anthropomorphize non-human entities. By exploring predefined, adaptive personas informed by user data, role-based approaches, historical and cultural influences, emotional support profiles, machine-learned personalization, and archetype-based models, this chapter explains various strategies for embedding human-like attributes into AI systems. These method-ologies empower AI to deliver contextually appropriate, engaging, and empathetic interactions. Through the application of psychological frameworks such as the Big Five personality traits and Jungian archetypes, the chapter emphasizes multidisci-plinary effort required for designing AI that builds emotional connections with users. Advancements in machine learning techniques, such as GANs and CVAEs, broaden the potential for AI to develop personalities that elevate user satisfaction and trust.

Keywords AI personas · Anthropomorphism · Artificial emotions (AE) · Character · Computational techniques · Emotional intelligence · Personality · Typology of chatbot persona

5.1 Introduction

The development of artificial intelligence (AI) has achieved monumental strides, with AI systems now capable of engaging in complex decision-making, emulating human-like interactions, and adapting to various contexts. One of the most compelling break-throughs in the field is the infusion of personality traits into AI endowing it with an ability to enact diverse societal roles. This desire to provide AI with personality traits originates from the ancient human tendency to anthropomorphize objects. Anthro-pomorphism, derived from the Greek words "Anthropos" (human) and "morphe" (form), reflects humans' innate predisposition to attribute human characteristics to non-human entities. This tendency is deeply rooted in human psychology and culture, fulfilling three primary human needs: the need for social connection, the need for understanding, and the need for control [3]. By assigning human-like qualities to

© The Author(s), under exclusive license to Springer Nature Switzerland AG 2025   49
G. Z. Karimova, *Humanizing AI with Personality*,
SpringerBriefs in Computer Science, https://doi.org/10.1007/978-3-031-82327-5_5

inanimate objects, people can create social relationships and communicate with these entities in a more meaningful and emotionally satisfying way [26].

AI agents featuring diverse social and psychological attributes, along with distinct personality traits, are being swiftly developed to augment the anthropomorphic characteristics [23]. While the anthropomorphism of AI service agents can also generate greater expectations for their abilities and adherence to social norms [7], AI agents with well-defined personality traits cultivate deeper user rapport and relatability. making interactions feel more natural, which leads to increased user satisfaction and trust in the system [2, 28].

Despite these developments, there remains a gap in understanding how structured AI personas, modeled after human personality traits, can be systematically created and utilized to improve human–machine interactions. This chapter addresses this gap by exploring the application of AI personalities.

5.2   AI Personas Versus AI Personality

AI personas and AI personalities are often used interchangeably, but they denote different aspects of AI design. An AI persona is a synthetic construct designed to emulate human-like characteristics and behaviors tailored for specific roles within AI systems [29]. It is a holistic representation that includes backstory, motivations, and personality traits. A persona for a conversational agent is a fabricated character that may include attributes such as a name, age, education or occupation, and even detailed background information and personality traits [17].

AI personality specifically refers to the individual traits and communication tendencies that an AI exhibits similar to human personality traits. While AI personas encompass a broader scope, including the personality, context, and function of the AI entity, AI personality focuses purely on the behavioral aspect.

While AI personality rests on the individual traits and communication styles that mirror human behaviors, AI personas offer a more comprehensive approach, integrating these personality traits with contextual and functional elements. Understanding the typologies of chatbot persona creation methods leads to the development of AI systems capable of delivering tailored and empathetic responses. Additionally, these typologies allow AI to meet specific user needs, adapt to varying scenarios, and maintain consistency in interactions (Fig. 5.1).

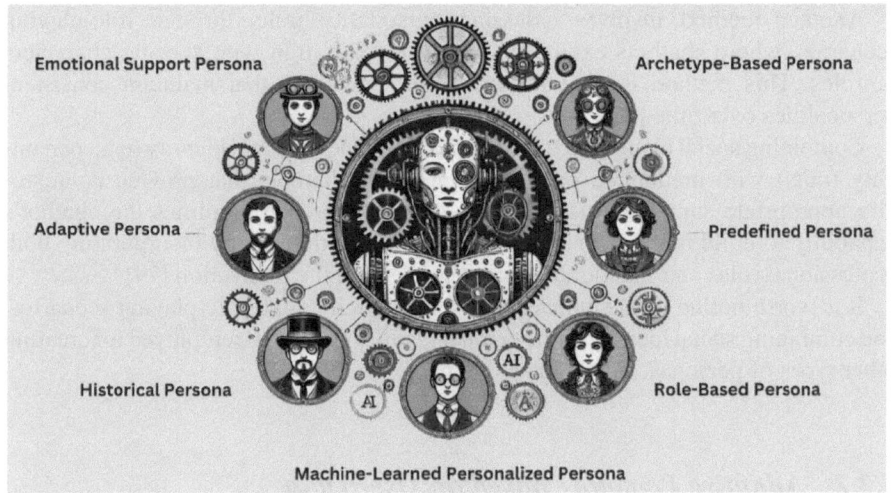

Fig. 5.1 The typology of chatbot persona. *Note* The figure was created using Dall-E and Canva

5.3 Typology of Chatbot Persona Creation Methods

5.3.1 Predefined Personas

Assigning predefined personas to chatbots allows the creation of more personalized responses [18, 22, 30]. Personality could be reflected in a few sentences or attributes, aiding chatbots in generating responses aligned with these personas. This method assigns fixed personality traits to chatbots, based on specific personality types or roles, providing a consistent but static user interaction experience. These traits are often described in text and help generate responses associated with the predefined persona.

Predefined personas for chatbots can be developed through several methods to create consistent and engaging user interactions. One effective approach involves the use of descriptive sentences and attribute-value pairs. For instance, defining a chatbot with sentences like "I am a young artist" or using attribute pairs such as {Gender: Female, Age: Young} can help shape the chatbot's personality, providing clear guidelines for consistent responses [24].

Another method employs templates and genre-specific text to generate predefined personas. Templates offer a structured format for the chatbot's replies, while genre text can invigorate the chatbot with specific personality traits relevant to the genre, such as romantic or mysterious themes [24]. Examples of predefined personas include a customer service chatbot with a polite and helpful demeanor, an educational chatbot designed to be knowledgeable and authoritative, and a healthcare chatbot characterized by compassion and support. These predefined personas anchor the chatbot's ability to deliver predictable and coherent interactions.

Another method involves assessing personality traits through role-playing scenarios, where chatbots exhibit personalities that align with specific characters or roles. This method is effective in creating chatbots that maintain consistent personalities over time [25].

Combining social identity (e.g., job or position) and personal identity (e.g., personality traits) with predefined personas can create chatbots that provide contextually appropriate support. This dualistic identity approach amplifies the chatbot's capability to build more meaningful relationships with users by incorporating both professional roles and individual characteristics into the interaction [29].

It is worth noting that templates and genre-specific text, role-playing scenarios, and combining social identity with personal identity can also be employed for creating other types of personas, such as adaptive personas.

5.3.2 Adaptive Personas Based on User Data

Chatbots with adaptive personas automatically learn the implicit user profile from the user's dialogue history and produce personalized responses based on this profile. Such chatbots can be customized based on a user's historical data. They can mimic the user's behavior, acting as their agent, and interacting with other users [14]. Users' historical data often reveal their language style, background knowledge, commonly used vocabulary and interests. There are two reasons why user dialogue history is more beneficial than explicit persona descriptions: it can be easily gathered on client devices and contains extensive personalized information, making it suitable for automatically learning user-profiles and generating personalized responses [14].

To further increase the adaptability and contextual relevance of chatbots, recent studies have developed techniques that blend elements of both predefined and adaptive personas. [12] proposed a Persona Retrieval Model (PRM) and a Posterior-Scored Transformer (PS-Transformer) to address the challenges when a chatbot's predefined persona does not cover certain conversation contexts. The PRM utilizes Natural Language Inference (NLI) models to extract relevant personas from a global collection, ensuring that the chatbot's responses remain consistent with predefined personas. Simultaneously, the PS-Transformer fine-tunes the application of these personas based on the actual conversation context, thus improving the chatbot's ability to handle unexpected queries effectively while maintaining a coherent persona [12]. This hybrid approach strengthens both the stability of predefined personas and the adaptability of responsive interactions. It offers a comprehensive solution for creating more responsive and context-aware chatbots.

Another approach for creating adaptive personas, as seen in [8], involves the Persona Enhanced Dual Alternating Learning Network (PEDNet). This approach employs two distinct networks: a Context-Dominant Network (CDNet) that confirms that responses are contextually relevant and a Persona-Dominate Network (PDNet) that focuses on integrating persona-specific information. By alternately training these networks, PEDNet can generate highly personalized responses that maintain the integrity of the predefined persona. This dual network system enables the chatbot to adapt its persona dynamically based on the interaction context, while still retaining the consistent traits of the predefined persona [8].

Recent advancements, such as ReferenceNet and Pose Guider, have improved the creation of AI personas by significantly increasing the consistency and realism of AI characters. These tools allow for the fine-tuning of AI interactions in response to user data, creating a more lifelike experience.

5.3.3 Role-Based Personas

Chatbots are designed for specific roles or identities, such as an expert, peer, or advisor, based on the context of interaction. This method heightens the chatbot's relevance by tailoring responses to fit its assigned role [5]. Role-based personas improve user satisfaction by guiding the chatbot to deliver contextually appropriate responses.

Examples of role-based personas include a customer service representative chatbot designed to handle customer queries and provide support, characterized by a helpful and patient demeanor; a technical support advisor chatbot tailored to offer detailed troubleshooting advice, showcasing expertise and precision; and an educational tutor chatbot focused on providing homework help and educational resources, demonstrating knowledge and authority. Such social roles ascribed to chatbots significantly affect the perceived bond between the user and the chatbot. The social role theory and social response theory indicate that chatbots impersonating different social roles can cater to user-specific needs, improving the overall user experience [16].

Modern chatbots can dynamically adapt their roles based on the interaction context. For instance, a chatbot might act as an advisor in one scenario and switch to a peer role in another, based on user inputs and situational demands. This flexibility allows the chatbot to remain relevant across different interactions [10].

5.3.4 Historical or Cultural Personas

Historical or cultural personas emulate well-known historical figures or archetypal characters from popular media, incorporating rich backstories and familiar traits. While this type might initially appear to fall under the category of role-based personas due to their character-driven nature, the key difference lies in their integration of historical and cultural narratives that add depth and authenticity to the interactions. Historical and cultural personas can represent both deceased and living figures, contributing to what is sometimes referred to as "virtual immortality" [21] when the personas imitate those who are no longer alive. Early systems that demonstrated the potential for conversations with historical figures such as Charles Darwin or

Richard Nixon were hand-engineered, supporting dialogue on a limited range of topics [19].

These early systems, while innovative, had limitations due to their reliance on pre-scripted dialogues and restricted conversational scope. However, advancements in artificial intelligence and machine learning have extended the capabilities of these personas. Modern approaches utilize natural language processing (NLP) techniques such as BERT (Bidirectional Encoder Representations from Transformers) and large-scale language models like OpenAI's GPT-3 (Generative Pre-trained Transformer 3) to create more interactive experiences.

The creation of historical or cultural personas involves using advanced natural language processing (NLP) techniques and machine learning models to accurately reflect the personality, language style, and knowledge base of the chosen historical figure or cultural archetype. For example, generative models like GPT-4 or newer iterations can be fine-tuned on texts and dialogues related to the persona, ensuring the chatbot can imitate the character convincingly. An educational chatbot adopting the persona of Albert Einstein could provide responses that blend humor and intellectual curiosity, distinctive of Einstein. Such a persona would deliver educational content and engage users through its relatable and familiar character traits [24]. Similarly, a travel chatbot embodying the persona of Marco Polo could offer rich, historically contextualized travel advice and anecdotes, making the interaction more captivating and informative.

5.3.5 Supportive Personas

Supportive personas are designed to provide contextually appropriate and relatable responses in scenarios where understanding and assistance are crucial, such as in mental health support or stress management. Unlike general role-based personas that focus solely on specific functions or tasks, supportive personas incorporate aspects of personal and social identities to resonate deeply with users. These personas are crafted to reflect a personality that conveys competence, care, and attentiveness, which are essential in providing comfort and reassurance in challenging situations.

The development of supportive personas often involves advanced natural language processing (NLP) techniques and machine learning models, such as recurrent neural networks (RNNs) and transformer models, which can be trained on extensive datasets of conversations. These models help in generating responses that align with the supportive and nurturing characteristics of the persona. For instance, a mental health chatbot might adopt a persona that blends professional competence with a caring attitude, making users feel understood and valued [29]. Another example could be a chatbot designed for grief support, which adopts a persona that offers comforting dialogue tailored to the needs of those coping with loss. This type of persona is particularly effective in creating a supportive environment where users feel safe expressing their concerns and seeking assistance.

Moreover, techniques like Persona Extraction through Semantic Similarity (PESS) can be employed to refine the consistency of supportive personas. This approach improves the chatbot's ability to maintain a consistent and reliable personality across interactions [6].

Further improvements can be achieved through the use of conversational models that are fine-tuned with persona-specific data, shaping the AI to produce responses that reflect a well-defined personality. For instance, the CoBERT model utilizes multi-hop co-attention mechanisms to generate responses that are in harmony with the persona's characteristics, thereby enhancing the user's experience by making the interactions feel more personal and relevant [31].

5.3.6 Machine-Learned Personalized Personas

Machine-learned personalized personas employ advanced machine-learning algorithms to develop chatbot personalities that are dynamically tailored to user interactions and contextual information. These personas are created using techniques that allow chatbots to adaptively generate responses based on multiple personal attributes, reflecting individual user preferences.

Techniques such as Generative Adversarial Networks (GANs) and Conditional Variational Autoencoders (CVAEs) allow for the creation of complex chatbot personas. These models can generate responses based on multiple personal attributes, offering fine-grained control over the chatbot's personality [13]. The Big Five or Five-Factor Model (FFM) is frequently employed in creating AI agents' personalities [25, 27].

Given the existence of various other personality assessment frameworks in psychology [4], these, too, have been utilized in the development of AI with distinct personalities [20, 1]. For example, the Myers-Briggs Type Indicator (MBTI) categorizes personalities into sixteen distinct types based on four dichotomies: extraversion-introversion, sensing-intuition, thinking-feeling, and judging-perceiving. Another notable framework is the HEXACO model, which extends the Big Five by adding a sixth dimension of honesty-humility [1]. The Enneagram, a model comprising nine interconnected personality types, has also been utilized to inform the development of AI personalities, emphasizing the dynamic and transformative aspects of personality [20]. The Big Five or the Five-Factor Model (FFM) has been used extensively to predict personality traits from textual data, aiding in the automatic generation of AI personas [15].

5.3.7 Archetype-Based Personas

Archetype-based personas employ Jungian archetypes to create chatbot personalities that resonate with deep-seated, universally recognized patterns of human behavior and thought. By aligning chatbot personas with well-known archetypes such as the Hero, the Caregiver, or the Explorer, developers can craft AI entities that evoke specific emotional and psychological responses from users [9]. This method utilizes well-known character tropes and historical figures to provide rich backstories and familiar archetypes.

Using familiar character tropes from popular media, such as the "Lovable Rogue" or "Retired Outlaw," helps in creating engaging and relatable chatbots. These tropes provide rich backstories and familiar archetypes that attract users. This method keeps chatbot responses consistent, helping create user interactions that appear personal and genuine [24]. Examples of archetype-based personas include the Hero Archetype, which is used to motivate users in a fitness app by encouraging them to achieve their goals and overcome challenges; the Caregiver Archetype, which provides emotional support in mental health applications by offering compassion and understanding to users in need; and the Explorer Archetype, which inspires users to explore new destinations and experiences in travel and adventure planning. Some conceptual frameworks map standard psychological and persona models to different kinds of agents' functionality [11]. Archetype classes can serve as starting points for designers and developers in building conversational agents.

5.4 Summary

In synthesizing the diverse methodologies for constructing AI personas, one discerns a considerable orientation toward the human inclination to imbue non-human entities with human-like qualities. This is why it is unsurprising that humans aspire to anthropomorphize AI-based conversational agents. Personas and personality assist in anthropomorphism by rendering AI interactions more relatable and engaging, thus engendering a sense of familiarity and trust. There are several methods for creating personas: predefined personas, adaptive personas based on user data, role-based personas, historical and cultural personas, emotional support personas, social identity and personal identity integration, and archetype-based personas.

Predefined personas provide consistent, albeit static, interaction experiences by assigning fixed personality traits based on specific roles, while adaptive personas utilize user data to dynamically personalize interactions, reflecting the unique behaviors and preferences of individual users. This adaptive approach exemplifies the technological strides in AI, where systems are endowed with the capability to evolve and respond in a more human-centric manner.

The integration of role-based personas accentuates the significance of context-specific interactions. Consider a chatbot that adeptly transitions from a knowledgeable advisor in a technical support scenario to a supportive peer in a mental health context, adapting its responses to the user's immediate needs. Historical or cultural personas emulate well-known figures from history and popular media, incorporating rich backstories and familiar traits. These personas inform and educate, offering contextually enriched interactions that connect the past with the present. Emotional support personas are crafted to provide empathetic replies, particularly in scenarios requiring emotional comfort or mental health support, utilizing sentiment analysis, emotional recognition algorithms, and advanced machine learning models. Moreover, by integrating social identity with personal identity, chatbots can offer a richer vicarious experience. For example, a healthcare chatbot might combine the professional conduct of a doctor with compassionate personal traits. Archetype-based personas draw from timeless character archetypes, such as the Hero, Caregiver, or Explorer to create AI personalities that evoke specific emotional responses. For example, a fitness app chatbot embodying the Hero archetype could motivate users by encouraging them to overcome challenges and achieve their goals, while an Explorer archetype in a travel app could inspire users to discover new destinations. These archetypal personas tap into universal human experiences, making interactions feel more intuitive.

By employing these diverse methodologies, AI developers can craft chatbots that are not only functional but also emotionally engaging and contextually adept.

In order to create such complex AI personas, developers can rely on advanced machine learning techniques, including Generative Adversarial Networks (GANs) and Conditional Variational Autoencoders (CVAEs). These technologies facilitate the embodiment of multifaceted personalities that exhibit subtle human traits.

There are various methodologies for assessing personalities, which can be effectively tested and utilized in designing AI agents. The use of psychological frameworks, such as the Big Five personality traits and Jungian archetypes, exemplifies the multidisciplinary approach necessary to create AI that establishes an emotional connection with users.

Reflecting on these advancements, it becomes evident that the task of creating AI with personality is both a technical challenge and a philosophical endeavor. By blending cutting-edge technology with deep psychological insights, we pave the way for AI systems that accomplish their missions and enrich human experience through authentic communications.

References

1. Ashton, M. C., Lee, K.: How well do big five measures capture HEXACO scale variance? J. Pers. Assess. **101**(6), 567–573 (2018). https://doi.org/10.1080/00223891.2018.1448986
2. Cai, N., Gao, S., & Yan, J.:How the communication style of chatbots influences consumers' satisfaction, trust, and engagement in the context of service failure. Humanit. Soc. Sci. Commun. **11**(1), 1–11 (2024)
3. Epley, N., Waytz, A., Cacioppo, J.T.: On seeing human: a three-factor theory of anthropomorphism. Psychol. Rev. **114**(4), 864–886 (2007)
4. Feher, A., Vernon, P.: Looking beyond the big five: a selective review of alternatives to the Big Five model of personality. Personality Individ. Differ. **169**, 110002 (2021). https://doi.org/10.1016/j.paid.2020.110002
5. Følstad, A., Brandtzæg, P.B.: Chatbots and the new world of HCI. Interactions **24**, 38–42 (2017)

6. Han, X., Wang, L., Li, Y., Zhang, W.: Persona extraction through semantic similarity for enhanced emotional support chatbots. J. Artif. Intell. Res. **72**, 123–145 (2024). https://doi.org/10.1016/j.jair.2024.115461

7. Huang, M.H., Rust, R.T.: Artificial intelligence in service. J. Serv. Res. **21**(2), 155–172 (2018)

8. Jiang, B., Zhou, W., Yang, J., Yang, C., Wang, S.: PEDNet: A persona-enhanced dual alternating learning network for conversational response generation. In: Proceedings of the 28th International Conference on Computational Linguistics (COLING 2020) (2020). https://doi.org/10.18653/V1/2020.COLING-MAIN.361

9. Karimova, G.Z., Goby, V.P.: The adaptation of anthropomorphism and archetypes for marketing artificial intelligence. J. Consum. Mark. **38**(2), 229–238 (2021). https://doi.org/10.1108/JCM-04-2020-3785

10. Kim, T., Molina, M. D., Rheu, M., Zhan, E. S., & Peng, W.: One AI does not fit all: A cluster analysis of the laypeople's perception of AI roles. In Proceedings of the 2023 CHI Conference on Human Factors in Computing Systems pp. 1–20 (2023)

11. Lessio, N., Morris, A.: Toward design archetypes for conversational agent personality. In: 2020 IEEE International Conference on Systems, Man, and Cybernetics (SMC), pp. 3221–3228 (2020). https://doi.org/10.1109/SMC42975.2020.9283254

12. Liu, Y., Wei, W., Liu, J., Mao, X., Fang, R., Chen, D.: Improving personality consistency in conversation by persona extending. In: *Proceedings of the 31st ACM International Conference on Information & Knowledge Management* (2022)

13. Lu, Z., Wei, W., Qu, X., Mao, X., Chen, D., & Chen, J.: MIRACLE: Towards personalized dialogue generation with latent-space multiple personal attribute control (2023). ArXiv preprint arXiv:2310.18342

14. Ma, Z., Dou, Z., Zhu, Y., Zhong, H., Wen, J.-R.: One chatbot per person: creating personalized chatbots based on implicit user profiles (2021). Retrieved from https://ar5iv.labs.arxiv.org/html/2108.09355

15. Mairesse, F., Walker, M. A., Mehl, M. R., Moore, R. K.: Using linguistic cues for the automatic recognition of personality in conversation and text. J. Artif. Intell. Res. **30**(1), 457–500 (2007)

16. Nißen, M., Rüegger, D., Stieger, M., Flückiger, C., Allemand, M., von Wangenheim, F., Kowatsch, T.: The effects of health care chatbot personas with different social roles on the client-chatbot bond and usage intentions. J. Med. Internet Res. **24**. (2022). https://doi.org/10.2196/32630

17. Pradhan, A., Lazar, A.: Hey Google, do you have a personality? Designing personality and personas for conversational agents. In: *CUI 2021 - 3rd Conference on Conversational User Interfaces (CUI '21)*, July 27–29, 2021, Bilbao (online), Spain. ACM, New York, NY, USA, 4 pages (2021). https://doi.org/10.1145/3469595.3469607

18. Qian, Q., Huang, M., Zhao, H., Xu, J., Zhu, X.: Assigning personality/profile to a chatting machine for coherent conversation generation. In: *Proceedings of the IJCAI 2018* (pp. 4279–4285) (2018)

19. Qian, X., Oard, D.W., Chan, J.: Conversational interaction with historical figures: what's it good for? In: *Proceedings of the International Conference on Human-Computer Interaction* (pp. 36–47). Springer-Verlag (2022). https://doi.org/10.1007/978-3-030-96960-8_3

20. Riso, D. R. & Hudson, R.:Personality types: Using the enneagram for self-discovery. Houghton Mifflin Company (1996)

21. Rothblatt, M.: Virtually Human: The Promise and the peril of digital immortality. St. Martin's Press, New York, NY (2014)

22. Song, H., Zhang, W.-N., et al.: Generating persona consistent dialogues by exploiting natural language inference. In: *Proceedings of the AAAI 2020* (pp. 8878–8885) (2020).

23. Spatola, N., Wykowska, A.: The personality of anthropomorphism: How the need for cognition and the need for closure define attitudes and anthropomorphic attributions toward robots. Comput. Hum. Behav. **122**, 106841 (2021). https://doi.org/10.1016/J.CHB.2021.106841

24. Sutcliffe, R.: A survey of personality, persona, and profile in conversational agents and chatbots (2024). Retrieved from https://ar5iv.labs.arxiv.org/html/2401.00609

25. Wang, X., Shi, W., Kim, R., Oh, Y., Yang, S., Zhang, J., Yu, Z.: Persuasion for good: towards a personalized persuasive dialogue system for social good (2023). ArXiv preprint arXiv:1906.06725.
26. Waytz, A., Cacioppo, J.T., Epley, N.: Who sees human? The stability and importance of individual differences in anthropomorphism. Perspect. Psychol. Sci. **5**(3), 219–232 (2010)
27. Xing, Y., Fernández, R.: Automatic evaluation of neural personality-based chatbots. (2018) ArXiv preprint arXiv:1810.00472.
28. Yang, Y., Liu, Y., Lv, X., Ai, J., Li, Y.: Anthropomorphism and customers' willingness to use artificial intelligence service agents. J. Hosp. Market. Manag. **31**(1), 1–23 (2021). https://doi.org/10.1080/19368623.2021.1926037
29. Yorita, A., Egerton, S., Chan, C., Kubota, N.: Chatbot persona selection methodology for emotional support. In: *2023 62nd Annual Conference of the Society of Instrument and Control Engineers (SICE)* (pp. 333–338) (2023). https://doi.org/10.23919/SICE59929.2023.10354130
30. Zhang, S., Dinan, E., Urbanek, J., Szlam, A., Kiela, D., Weston, J.: Personalizing dialogue agents: I have a dog, do you have pets too? In: *Proceedings of the ACL 2018* (pp. 2204–2213). ACL (2018).
31. Zhong, P., Zhang, C., Wang, H., Liu, Y., Miao, C.: Towards persona-based empathetic conversational models. In: Proceedings of the 2020 Conference on Empirical Methods in Natural Language Processing (EMNLP), pp. 292–303, (2020)

Chapter 6
Designing the Appearance of Conversational Agents with Personality

Abstract This chapter explores the design principles for crafting the 'appearance' of conversational agents endowed with personality. Unlike physical robots, the appearance of chatbots is conveyed through a range of non-physical elements—voice, language style, visual interface, and conversational flow—that collectively shape their persona. Drawing from personality-grounded frameworks and design theories, the chapter introduces a comprehensive framework that integrates concepts from user-centered design, affective computing, personality psychology (including the Big Five traits), and brand identity to create consistent and engaging interactions. A mapping of personality traits to design components is provided, depicting how voice tone, linguistic style, visual branding, and emotional resonance impact user perception. Emphasizing stakeholder-centric design, the chapter presents guidelines and best practices for developing conversational agents that align with organizational values and user expectations. Through this framework, practitioners are equipped to deepen the emotional connection of their chatbots, whether AI-driven or rule-based, by thoughtfully integrating design elements that bring the agent's personality to life.

Keywords AI personas · Aesthetic overshadowing · Affective computing · Archetypes · Conversational design · Personality framework · Stakeholders · User-centered design · Vampire effect

6.1 Introduction

Creating a conversational agent (CA) with personality is a peculiar exercise. Here lies a task of sculpting character out of words, tone, and pauses. Unlike the static machines of yesterday, these agents are brought to life by language, molded to mimic the most human of behaviors: conversation [17].

What truly makes this endeavor fascinating is the human propensity to see machines not as lines of code or sequences of commands but as social beings. Our minds instinctively treat computers, even those speaking only in text, as social actors [42]. Thus, the 'appearance' of a CA is not a question of pixels or polygons, but rather

© The Author(s), under exclusive license to Springer Nature Switzerland AG 2025   61
G. Z. Karimova, *Humanizing AI with Personality*,
SpringerBriefs in Computer Science, https://doi.org/10.1007/978-3-031-82327-5_6

the shaping of voice, vocabulary, and responsiveness. In short, it is not a physical appearance that we are constructing, but a behavioral one.

Each choice—whether in phrasing, rhythm, or response time—has profound implications. A conversational agent with a quick, informal reply can exude friendliness but risk triviality. Meanwhile, one with measured pauses and formal language might project competence but lack warmth [8]. It is a delicate exercise of balance, where every word, intonation, and silence are part of a calculated persona that radiates human social dynamics and expectations [7].

In designing such an entity, one does not simply code responses; one curates experiences, engineers social presence, and—if done artfully—creates an agent that speaks, listens, and feels alive. To achieve this, the development of conversational agents (CAs) endowed with personality requires the integration of multiple theoretical perspectives. Such frameworks guide these entities beyond basic functionality toward meaningful user engagement. Unlike traditional interfaces, CAs are crafted to exhibit characteristics that create an impression of human-like presence. This presence is achieved through a compilation of verbal, auditory, and visual cues that together shape how the agent is perceived and interacted with.

To construct CAs that embody personality effectively, we must analyze several theoretical frameworks, including User-Centered Design (UCD), affective computing, personality theories like the Big Five, brand identity theories, and frameworks, addressing social presence and interaction dynamics, which collectively shape how CAs resonate with their users.

Central to this endeavor is User-Centered Design, which emphasizes tailoring design elements to users' needs, behaviors, and preferences [36, 2, 20]. Within the context of CAs, UCD serves as a critical foundation for shaping responses, dialogue styles, and interaction mechanisms that align with users' cognitive frameworks [15], rendering interactions more intuitive and familiar.

The emotional dimension of interaction is further explored through the principles of affective computing and emotional design [37, 40]. These theories posit that human–machine exchanges are greatly improved when systems are capable of detecting, interpreting, and adapting to the user's emotional state [26]. A chatbot's design, therefore, must encompass more than simple dialogues—it requires an understanding of how language, tone, and auditory patterns can evoke the desired emotional response.

Personality theories, notably the Big Five Personality Traits and the Myers-Briggs Type Indicator, offer a structured approach for mapping specific personality traits onto design elements [39]. For example, an agent characterized by extraversion might use expressive language and rapid dialogue, while one aligned with conscientiousness might communicate in a precise and reserved manner. These personality constructs allow for the development of agents whose behavioral styles are consistent and tailored to their intended roles.

Kapferer's Brand Identity Prism [24] offers an additional perspective, positing that the CA's appearance and communication style must mirror the broader identity of the brand it represents. The agent's linguistic choices, voice modulation, and visual branding elements work in concert to reflect the brand's values and ethos, crafting a cohesive user experience that reinforces the intended brand image [28].

The concept of social presence, derived from Social Presence Theory [45], adds another layer to CA design. Social presence concerns how 'real' an agent feels in mediated communication, influencing the user's perception of trustworthiness and authenticity. A CA that skillfully manages timing, voice tone, and conversational cues can elicit a stronger impression of being a present and attentive interlocutor.

Lastly, the Personality-Grounded Framework [24] advances an approach to designing the appearance of AI products, distinguishing between perceived physical and expressive dimensions. The framework identifies six core dimensions—color tone, sound/speech/voice, movement/gestures/facial expressions, clothes/texture, shape/size, and smell—which jointly shape how a conversational agent's personality and purpose can be communicated. Importantly, this approach emphasizes that the design must align with not only the agent's intended archetype but also its functional purpose. The aim is to evoke contextually appropriate emotional responses from stakeholders, which may range from trust and familiarity to authority or fear, depending on the desired relationship between the agent and its audience [24]. Thus, stakeholder expectations and the CA's role are central in determining how these dimensions are combined to achieve a consistent and effective persona.

These theories form a blueprint for the design of CAs that are not just utilitarian but are also engaging, relatable, and effective communicators. The subsequent sections will examine how these theoretical keystones translate into practice, offering detailed insights into building CAs whose persona aligns with stakeholders' expectations, emotions, contextual demands and brand image.

6.2   A Unified Framework for Crafting Chatbot Personalities

The creation of a chatbot with personality is not simply about coding responses or designing a user-friendly interface; it is about developing a cohesive entity that feels both authentic and purpose-driven. To achieve this, one must craft a comprehensive framework that synthesizes theories on personality, design, and user interaction. At the core of this approach is the understanding that a chatbot's personality emerges from a combination of verbal, auditory, and visual elements, shaped and constrained by the context in which it is meant to operate. This section outlines a comprehensive framework that integrates the most relevant aspects of personality-grounded theory, UCD, affective computing, brand identity concepts, and established personality models.

The foundation of this framework begins with establishing a distinct persona for the chatbot. However, to comprehend what the 'persona' entails, one must first distinguish between personality types and archetypes, as each contributes differently to the chatbot's design and functionality. Personality types, modeled by theories like the Big

Five (OCEAN), break down traits into specific attributes such as openness, conscientiousness, extraversion, agreeableness, and neuroticism. These characteristics give depth to the chatbot's behavior, dictating how it communicates, responds, and adapts to users' needs. A chatbot high in extraversion, for example, might have an energetic and proactive conversational style, engaging users with enthusiasm, while one with high conscientiousness would provide thorough, structured, and accurate responses, accenting clarity and reliability. Thus, personality traits give the chatbot a finely tuned spectrum of behaviors, directly informing how it interacts at a micro-level in its day-to-day conversations.

Archetypes, on the other hand, represent broader thematic templates. Rooted in both psychological theory and brand identity frameworks, archetypes like the hero, sage, or caregiver shape not just how a chatbot communicates but the overarching role it plays and the emotional connection it forms with users. An archetype functions as a conceptual anchor, providing a holistic direction for how the chatbot's persona will manifest. For instance, a chatbot embodying the sage archetype may assume a role of wisdom and authority, offering guidance and thoughtful reflections, while a caregiver chatbot would focus on nurturing and empathetic interactions. The archetype serves as the overarching narrative or character blueprint that remains consistent across all interactions, guiding both verbal and visual cues.

The integration of both personality traits and archetypes within the framework allows for a coherent chatbot persona. While the archetype gives the chatbot its thematic identity and role, the specific personality traits add texture, guiding how that archetype is expressed in real-world scenarios. For instance, a chatbot with a sage archetype and a personality profile high in agreeableness might offer advice in a friendly, supportive manner, while one high in conscientiousness may emphasize clarity and structured reasoning in its guidance. The careful balance of both dimensions also complied maintains a consistent character that is also flexible enough to adapt to different conversational contexts.

Within this framework, UCD is essential for shaping how the chatbot's personality aligns with user needs and expectations. UCD emphasizes a deep understanding of different stakeholders, including end-users, clients, and designers, whose perspectives will inform the chatbot's role and conversational style. By assessing the user's emotional states, cultural context, and functional requirements, designers can tailor the chatbot's persona to be more intuitive and contextually relevant. For instance, a chatbot designed for healthcare support may require a personality that balances professionalism with empathy, while a chatbot for entertainment purposes might adopt a more playful and dynamic approach.

Beyond the personality and archetypal foundations lies the concept of appearance, which is not limited to the visual interface but includes voice, language style, and behavior [33]. In visualized chatbots, elements such as avatars, color schemes, and typography affect the chatbot's perception [27]. For voice-based chatbots, vocal qualities such as tone, accent, pitch, and speech rate shape the emotional tone of the interaction and affects user engagement [48]. These elements must align with the archetype and personality traits to present a coherent audio-visual identity.

The interaction style of the chatbot is further refined by applying principles from affective computing and social presence theories. A chatbot's skill in forming emotional bonds depends on how it employs conversational cues, such as empathic phrasing, active listening, and adaptive language [4]. The chatbot should be designed to identify and appropriately respond to the emotional state of the user, enhancing the interaction's depth and creating a sense of social presence.

Incorporating affective elements requires attention to the structure of conversation. The rhythm, timing, and choice of words can greatly influence how a user perceives the chatbot's personality [12]. The conversational flow must align with the archetype and personality traits established earlier, to retain authentic interaction. An extraverted chatbot, for instance, may employ quick, enthusiastic responses, while a more contemplative chatbot might pause before offering thoughtful insights.

Central to the framework is also the ongoing evaluation and iteration of the chatbot's design. By collecting user feedback and observing interaction patterns, designers can refine the chatbot's persona to better meet stakeholder needs and improve user satisfaction. This iterative process supports the chatbot's evolution, keeping it relevant.

The comprehensive framework thus integrates multiple dimensions—personality traits, archetypes, user-centered principles, affective cues, and appearance elements—to shape a chatbot that is not just functional but genuinely engaging, responsive, and reflective of its intended character.

The diagrammatic representation (Fig. 6.1) captures the essence of how personality traits, user-centered design principles, and affective design elements coalesce, ultimately resulting in a cohesive chatbot persona. It brings together the foundational personality constructs (derived from established typologies and archetypes), the translation of these constructs into design elements, and the iterative process that shapes the chatbot's final form. Each layer, from the core personality foundation to the peripheral evaluation and iterative design elements, plays a role in constructing a chatbot experience.

6.3 Defining the Personality Foundation

Personality defines how a chatbot interacts, making the encounter with the user more personalized and human-like. The starting point is to recognize that crafting a chatbot with personality requires integrating both personality trait models and archetypes. This integration must strike a balance between user expectations and desired character consistency.

The Big Five (OCEAN) model is frequently employed to provide a structured framework for personality. The model consists of five key dimensions: openness, conscientiousness, extraversion, agreeableness, and neuroticism [21]. By applying these dimensions to a chatbot's interactions, designers can craft responses that mirror human characteristics, ensuring the chatbot's behavior aligns with the selected traits. For example, a chatbot high in openness might employ more creative language and

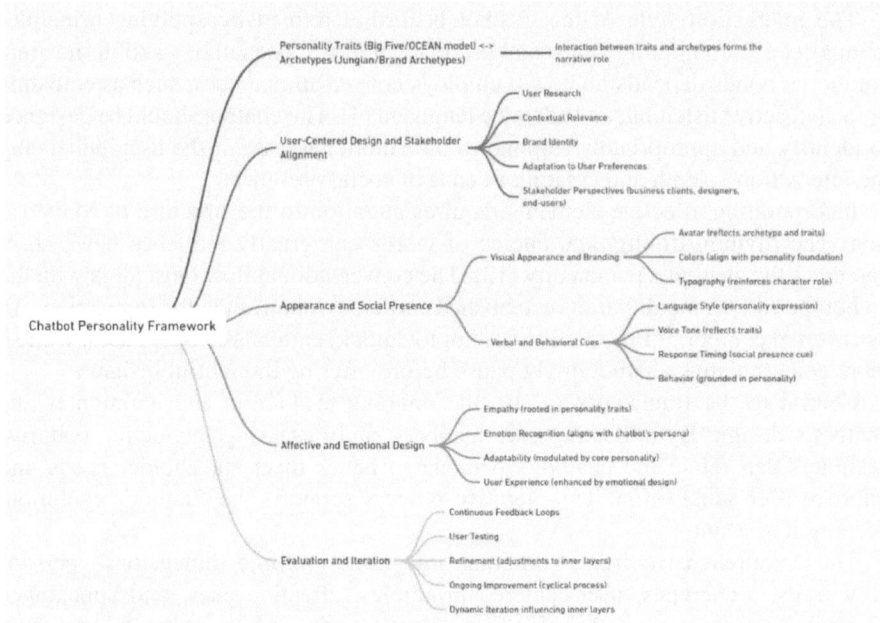

Fig. 6.1 Chatbot Personality Framework. *Note* The figure was created using Whimsical Diagrams

be open to diverse conversational topics, while one low in neuroticism will present more stable and reassuring responses.

In parallel to personality traits, archetypes provide broad templates for personas. Drawing inspiration from narrative themes, archetypes such as the sage, explorer, or caregiver offer foundational character sketches that resonate across various contexts [34]. By embedding these archetypes, a chatbot can manifest specific thematic roles, effectively engaging users through familiar character tropes. For instance, an explorer chatbot may exhibit curiosity in its dialogue, guiding users through exploratory questions and adventure-like scenarios.

The challenge lies in harmonizing granular personality traits with overarching archetypes to form a consistent and compelling character. For example, while the Big Five model lends specificity (e.g., high extraversion for a chatty bot), the archetype provides the foundational narrative (e.g., the entertainer). By synchronizing the OCEAN dimensions with the archetypal framework, the chatbot's individual traits are designed to complement its broader role, enriching its thematic expression. Ultimately, a well-crafted chatbot's persona is the outcome of a dual-layer process: defining the foundational traits through personality dimensions and embedding them within the framework of an archetype. This integrated approach keeps the chatbot coherent, engaging, and contextually appropriate, adjusting its conversational flow while maintaining its core character.

6.4 Engaging Stakeholders

This section addresses the often conflicting viewpoints of stakeholders, whose voices shape the very architecture and behavior of chatbots. Stakeholders, such as developers, corporate leaders, ethics advocates, regulators, and end-users, each impose unique demands on the design. These competing pressures must be intertwined into a coherent system that is not only practical but ethically robust. Such influences, from the uncompromising scrutiny of ethics panels to the utilitarian concerns of industry leaders, form a complex network of priorities.

At the heart of this inquiry lies the polyphonic model [24], a conceptual tool reengineered to address the design of chatbots with personality. In contrast to conventional AI systems, which may operate mechanically, chatbots endowed with personality occupy a more layered environment, where each participant—developers, investors, users, compliance officers, regulators, UX/UI designers, legal experts, business analysts, marketers, AI specialists, data scientists, product managers, and others—inscribes their own biases and expectations onto the system (Fig. 6.2.). The chatbot, in response, becomes not merely a passive receiver but an entity that evolves according to the shifting inputs of its creators and users.

An important shift in this model, when applied to chatbots with personality, is the recognition that the chatbot itself becomes an active contributor in the conversation. As users interact with it, the chatbot learns and adapts. While it may begin with a predefined personality, over time, this personality evolves, reflecting the exchanges it participates in. The chatbot's persona thus becomes a shared creation, reflecting the intentions of its designers as well as the behaviors and preferences of its users. This

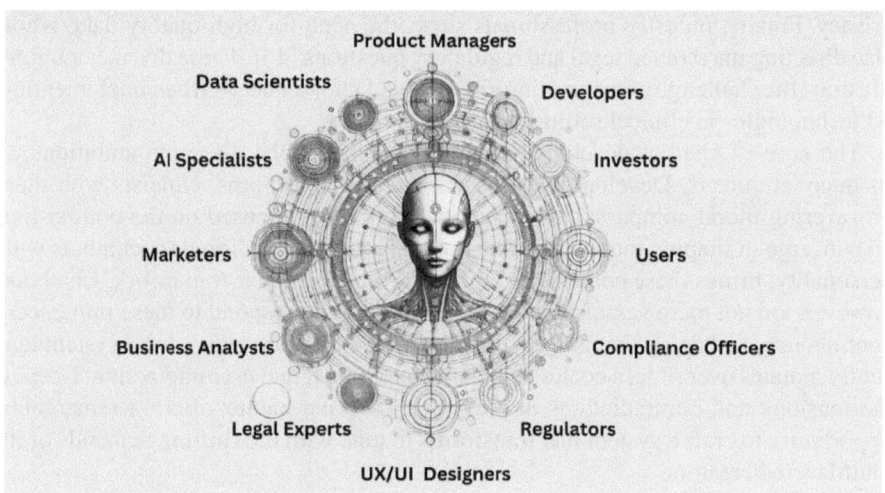

Fig. 6.2 Key Stakeholders for Chatbot Creation. *Note* The figure was created using DALL-E, Pixelcut, and Canva

back-and-forth relationship allows the chatbot to adapt, becoming a more responsive tool shaped by the conversations that surround it.

Experts have long pointed out the differing perceptions of stakeholders when assessing AI-driven entities. For example, the varying reactions were observed toward the humanoid robot Pepper, deployed in a commercial environment Niemelä et al. [35]. Customers, drawn by its interactive capabilities, found the robot engaging, describing it as "entertaining and useful" (Niemelä et al. 35, p. 119). Yet, mall managers were more concerned with the long-term financial implications of introducing such technology, particularly the costs and operational sustainability. This divergence in priorities points to the precarious balance in chatbot design—what captivates users may leave those responsible for its execution feeling unsettled.

A similar case is demonstrated in the hospitality industry, where service robots have drawn both praise and skepticism. Hotel guests were charmed by the robots' efficiency, viewing them as a valuable addition to their experience while hotel management weighed the technological and economic burdens, questioning the feasibility of large-scale implementation [47]. Such discord is not unique to humanoid robots but applies equally to conversational agents, where stakeholders' goals often pull in opposite directions.

A collage of opinions was also compiled when examining stakeholder perspectives on the integration of chatbots in healthcare [43]. Clinicians prioritize improved diagnostic accuracy and the reduction of mundane administrative tasks. However, they also express concerns over liability, privacy risks, and the erosion of empathy in patient care. Consumers, on the other hand, appreciate the accessibility of AI-powered chatbots but fear a loss of personal connection with their healthcare providers. Healthcare executives view AI through the lens of operational efficiency and cost-saving potential yet remain cautious about patient satisfaction and data privacy. Finally, industry professionals stress the need for high-quality data, while also directing unresolved legal and regulatory questions [46]. These diverse opinions illustrate the challenge of reconciling different stakeholder needs when implementing AI technologies in clinical settings [43].

The core of chatbot development lies in balancing the disparate ambitions of its many architects. Developers, with their precise algorithms, ethicists with their unwavering moral compass, and corporate pragmatists focused on the bottom line all converge in shaping the system. The polyphonic model, tailored for chatbots with personality, brings these contrasting ambitions into a singular framework. Chatbots, however, are not mere vessels; they actively absorb and respond to these influences, continuously reshaping themselves. The result is not a static entity, but a system that subtly mutates over time, a coalescence of creator intent and user interaction. Despite the tensions and contradictions at play, this adaptive nature offers a remarkable opportunity to craft a system that transforms in tune with the shifting demands of its multifaceted creators.

6.5 Crafting Appearance and Social Presence

Having addressed the deeper layers of stakeholder influence, we now shift to the outermost shell of the chatbot—the form in which it is presented to its users and the social cues it emits. A chatbot's appearance, be it graphical or textual, serves as the gateway to interaction. In nature, even the subtlest of visual details can be the difference between attraction and avoidance. The chatbot, too, must tread a fine line. Too mechanical an appearance might evoke feelings of distance or coldness, while an excessively human-like interface risks unsettling users, provoking an eerie sense of false familiarity—a phenomenon known as the 'uncanny valley' [32].

A chatbot's voice is one of the critical aspects of its perceived personality. Whether through spoken language in voice-based agents or written text in chat-based systems, the way a chatbot communicates deeply influences user perception. Research has demonstrated that factors like tone of voice, speech rate, and vocal warmth play a crucial role in shaping how users feel about interacting with a chatbot [13]. For example, a chatbot with a fast, lively tone might be perceived as energetic and engaging, while one with a slower, more deliberate speech pattern could be seen as thoughtful or authoritative [8].

More profound than mere appearance, however, is the notion of social presence— the degree to which an individual perceives another as 'present' or salient during an interaction [5] or the impression of a real, socially aware being lurking behind the screen. Highly anthropomorphic visual cues, such as a human figure, can increase the salience of the 'other person' more than low anthropomorphic visual cues, such as a bubble, because "the presence of a human figure attached to a chat agent itself can be suggestive of the existence of the 'other person' in the interaction" [16, p. 305].

The degree of anthropomorphism in chatbot design stretches across a continuum, from starkly mechanical entities to those imbued with lifelike characteristics that evoke human qualities. At the lower end, chatbots present as inanimate objects, governed by features such as color, movement, sound, language, shape, and size. These rudimentary elements emphasize function over form, evoking the cold efficiency of machines devoid of personal identity or emotional resonance. Their simplicity serves the purpose of functionality, requiring no interaction beyond mere command execution.

As we ascend towards more humanized representations, the elements of the chatbot's appearance slide to more elaborate and expressive dimensions. The introduction of gestures, facial expressions, and voice modulations ushers the chatbot into the realm of human mimicry [9]. Features such as clothing, height, and even cultural markers like nationality, age, and gender are crafted to engender an impression of relatability [24, p. 1691].

At the pinnacle of this spectrum, chatbots when embodied in physical forms like robots can resemble near-human beings, complete with facial movements, eye contact, and even simulated elements like fragrance or attire, all of which are intended to evoke a response that transcends the purely functional.

Surprisingly, even a chatbot's name holds a curious place on the spectrum of anthropomorphism [16]. While one might expect the physical design, facial expressions, or tone of conversation to define a chatbot's humanness, a seemingly innocuous factor such as its name can tip the balance. Human names like Elisa or Sophia naturally lead users to attribute human qualities to the chatbot, invoking preconceived notions even before any interaction begins [16]. Chatbots with human-like names increased emotional connection with users, purely based on this initial label [3]. In contrast, chatbots named E-12 or Data occupy the opposite end of this spectrum, signaling their more mechanical and utilitarian purpose, discouraging expectations of warmth or human-style conversation.

The name becomes a conduit through which users mentally anthropomorphize the chatbot, projecting human-like attributes onto it long before it responds with words or actions

Yet, as with all finely crafted entities, the appearance of the chatbot comes with risks. As designers push for more engaging and aesthetically rich experiences, they may unintentionally overstep into a phenomenon I shall term aesthetic overshadowing. Aesthetic overshadowing can be defined as a phenomenon in chatbot design where engaging or visually striking features become so dominant that they distract users from the chatbot's primary functionality or purpose. This phenomenon bears an inexplicable resemblance to the 'vampire effect' in advertising, where the seductive brilliance of a feature eclipses the very message it was designed to convey. In essence, the striking component, such as a celebrity endorsement or visually stunning feature, becomes so dominant that it 'sucks the life' out of the message, leaving the core purpose overshadowed. This concept has clear applications in chatbot design, where certain features may be so attention-grabbing that they detract from the chatbot's functional role.

When applied to chatbots, the concept of aesthetic overshadowing describes how certain captivating features can dominate user attention to such an extent that they detract from the chatbot's primary functionality. These distractions may take many forms. For example, humor—while superbly adept at drawing users into the interaction—can all too easily divert the conversation into the realm of frivolity, derailing the very tasks it was designed to facilitate [38].

Visual cues do far more than lure the user into a shallow distraction; they may evoke a host of unintended emotional responses, such as frustration, disappointment, or even anger [10]. Such distractions not only risk undermining the bot's utility but also harm the perception of the brand, eroding customer loyalty when users' expectations for task completion are not met [18].

The difficulty, therefore, lies in balancing these engaging elements so that they elevate, rather than detract from, the chatbot's operational goals. Aesthetic overshadowing serves as a cautionary tale, reminding us that while appearance and social presence are critical to the chatbot's success, they must never outshine its primary function. Designers must wield these features with the precision of an artist, careful not to let the overzealous brushstrokes of humor, visual effects, anthropomorphic cues [16], customizable backgrounds, playful avatars, facial expressions, peripheral

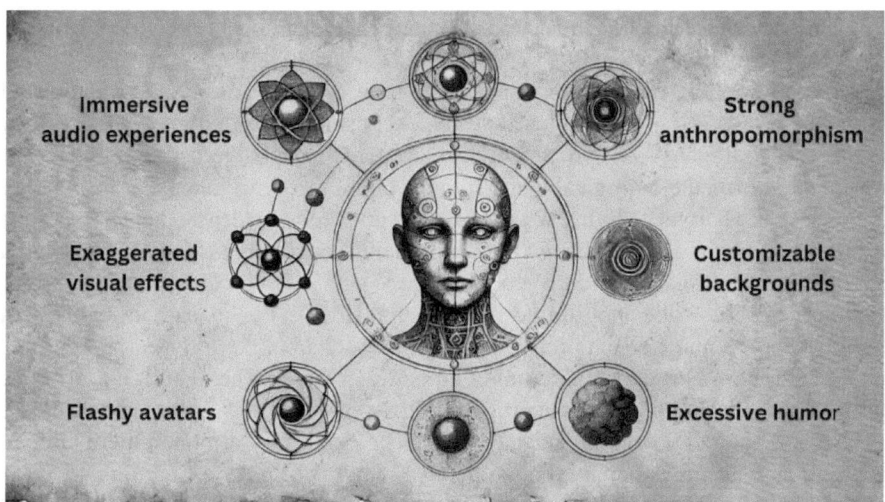

Fig. 6.3 Potential Contributors to the Aesthetic Overshadowing in Chatbots. *Note* The figure was created using DALL-E, Microsoft Photos, and Canva

visual cues (notifications or animations), and immersive audio experiences (sound effects) obscure the canvas of utility (Fig. 6.3.).

The visual design of a chatbot extends across a range, from color, texture, and movement, to gestures, facial expressions, and identity markers like age or gender. On one end, the chatbot is perceived as purely functional, while on the other, it takes on human-like qualities. Yet, the overuse of these visual elements risks what we might call 'aesthetic overshadowing'—where ostentatious visuals, animations, or ornate personalization steal focus from the chatbot's main purpose. This can leave users frustrated and harm their perception of the brand. The real challenge in crafting a chatbot's appearance is not in the mere selection of visual effects or animations, but in understanding the precise emotional response one seeks to provoke—whether it be amusement, empathy, or introspection—so that every element reflects the bot's role, be it to entertain, inform, or stir deeper emotional involvement.

6.6 Designing Affective and Emotional Dimensions

In the next layer of our framework, the emotional and affective dimensions of chatbot design are explored. While previous sections have discussed the outward appearance and social presence of chatbots, it is the emotional and affective properties that form the core of user trust. Studies show that participants often perceive human service agents as more competent and warmer than chatbots delivering the same service [30], underlining the need to design chatbots that resonate emotionally. To achieve this, the chatbot's behavior must be calibrated to evoke specific feelings in users, transcending mere functionality.

This requires a deeper understanding of how systems can evolve, adapt, and refine their responses—principles that are encapsulated in ontogeny. In artificial intelligence, ontogeny—the process of development through interaction—finds itself transplanted from the biological world into the circuitry of machines. Far from being confined to the habitat of living organisms, this concept now drives the very essence of how AI systems evolve, using "a developmental encoding scheme to translate a given genotype into a complete agent" [6, p. 237].

But this process does not unfold in an instant (Fig. 6.4.). Instead, it begins with the most rudimentary of emotional scaffolding: a chatbot starts with a predefined emotional tone—a crude simulacrum of empathy or cheerfulness, built into its code like a clockwork automaton mimicking life. These early responses, while serviceable, are mechanical and devoid of true emotions. The chatbot is, at first, a mere puppet, its emotional strings pulled by the predictable patterns of its programming.

However, as it interacts with users, a transformation begins. Using Natural Language Processing (NLP), the chatbot starts to perceive the emotional undercurrents of user inputs, much like a sailor learning to read the winds that guide his course. These emotional cues—whether embedded in a single word or threaded through the cadence of a conversation—become the raw material for the AI's emotional education [19].

And here is where the essence of emotional ontogeny truly unfolds. Emotional ontogeny is the developmental process by which a chatbot or artificial agent improves its ability to recognize, interpret, and respond to human emotions over time through interactions and learning. Through reinforcement learning [1, 11], evolutionary algorithms for emotional adaptation [6], affective neural networks [44], deep learning for

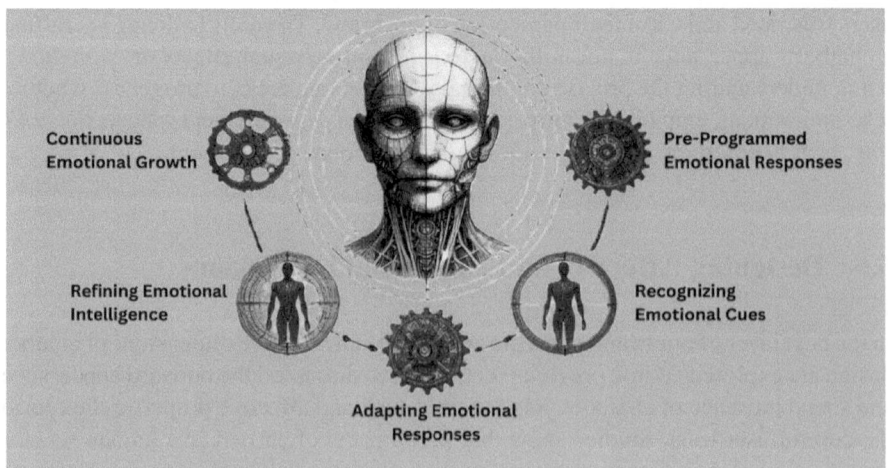

Fig. 6.4 Stages of Emotional Growth in AI Chatbots. *Note* The figure was created using DALL-E, Microsoft Photos, and Canva

emotion recognition [29], and emotional state machines [22, 31] the chatbot is no longer bound to its initial programming. It learns, much as a child learns the subtleties of social interaction, refining its emotional responses through continuous feedback and interaction. Positive feedback from users acts as the reward mechanism, subtly guiding the chatbot to refine its emotional responses. Over time, the AI's emotional repertoire expands, acquiring the grace to modulate its tone, its timing, even its choice of words, to better suit the emotional timbre of its interlocutors.

Now, this process is not a one-way street. As the chatbot's emotional intelligence grows, something curious happens: users begin to mirror the chatbot's emotional expressions. A chatbot designed for healthcare, for example, might respond to distress with calm, measured empathy, and soon enough, the user begins to reflect that calmness. It is a strange, almost symbiotic relationship, where human and machine emotions feed off one another, not unlike the way a flower and its pollinator evolve in tandem, each shaping the other through the slow, relentless forces of co-evolution [25].

Finally, through the relentless grind of interaction, the chatbot's emotional responses are refined over time, much as natural selection chisels away at the rough edges of a species, honing it into a form more perfectly suited to its environment. What began as a rudimentary imitation of emotion becomes, through countless iterations, a more genuine facsimile of emotional intelligence. The chatbot, once a marionette of pre-programmed behaviors, now exhibits something approaching emotional growth, a simulacrum of empathy forged not from mere code but from the crucible of experience [14].

In conclusion, the emotional and affective dimensions of chatbot design elevate the machine beyond its mechanical origins. The process of emotional ontogeny transforms these systems from static, pre-programmed entities into dynamic agents of interaction, capable of learning, adapting, and responding to the subtle ebbs and flows of human emotion. Much like nature's slow but relentless refinement of species, chatbots evolve, sharpening their emotional acuity with each user interaction.

6.7   Iterative Development and Feedback Loops

The final layer is indispensable, safeguarding the perpetual refinement and evolution of chatbots with personality. These feedback loops harvest data from user interactions, employing methods such as sentiment analysis and various engagement measures (e.g., response time, user satisfaction ratings, conversation length, and interaction frequency) to scrutinize the chatbot's efficacy. For instance, if users respond positively to empathetic responses, the chatbot's algorithms can prioritize similar emotional tones in future interactions. Research shows that sentiment analysis permits chatbots to become more attuned to user emotions [41].

By incorporating machine learning and Natural Language Processing (NLP), chatbots can swiftly polish their replies in a meaningful way. NLP grants the chatbot the ability to detect subtle conversational cues and strike an emotional chord with users. This adaptability is especially important in settings like healthcare or customer service, where user emotions can fluctuate. In such environments, real-time adjustments based on feedback allow for more emotionally aligned conversations [22].

6.8 Summary

This chapter presents a comprehensive, multi-layered framework for creating chatbots imbued with personality, addressing both their practical functionality and emotional depth. The foundation begins with user-centered design, accentuating the customization of chatbot interactions to users' needs, behaviors, and preferences. Subsequently, the discussion examines personality traits and archetypes, such as those derived from the Big Five personality model. By plotting distinct personality features onto design elements, the chatbot's persona becomes more coherent and relatable. An essential aspect explored is appearance and social presence, where the chatbot's voice, tone, visual design, and conversational style converge to create a cohesive persona. The chapter contemplates the roles of stakeholders, recognizing the diverse perspectives of developers, users, corporate leaders, and others involved in the chatbot's creation through approaches like the 'polyphonic model.' The final layer—iterative development and feedback loops—supports the refinement of chatbots over time through continuous learning from user interactions. By employing techniques such as sentiment analysis and machine learning, chatbots can adapt their responses to better meet user needs.

This stratified framework provides a clear methodology for developing chatbots that are operationally effective but also emotionally engaging, with polished personality traits and a compelling social presence that evolve through interaction and adaptation. By integrating design elements and continually improving through user feedback, practitioners can create conversational agents that effectively correspond with stakeholder expectations.

References

1. Ahmad, M.I., Gao, Y., Alnajjar, F., Shahid, S., Mubin, O.: Emotion and memory model for social robots: a reinforcement learning based behaviour selection. Behav. Inf. Tech. **41**(15), 3210–3236 (2021). https://doi.org/10.1080/0144929X.2021.1977389
2. Alves, T., Natálio, J., Henriques-Calado, J., Gama, S.: Incorporating personality in user interface design: a review. Personal. Ind. Differ. **155**(2020), 109709 (2020). https://doi.org/10.1016/j.paid.2019.109709
3. Araujo, T.: Living up to the chatbot hype: The influence of anthropomorphic design cues and communicative agency framing on conversational agent and company perceptions. Comput. Hum. Behav. **85**, 183–189 (2018)

4. Bilquise, G., Ibrahim, S., Shaalan, K.: Emotionally intelligent chatbots: a systematic literature review. Human Behav. Emerg. Technol. **2022**(1), 9601630 (2022). https://doi.org/10.1155/2022/9601630

5. Biocca, F., Harms, C., Burgoon, J.K.: Toward a more robust theory and measure of social presence: review and suggested criteria. Presence: Teleoperators Virt. Environ. **12**(5), 456–480. https://doi.org/10.1162/105474603322761270

6. Bongard, J. C., Pfeifer, R.: Evolving complete agents using artificial ontogeny. In: Hara, F., Pfeifer, R. (eds) Morpho-Functional Machines: The New Species. Springer, Tokyo (2003). https://doi.org/10.1007/978-4-431-67869-4_12

7. Brave, S., Nass, C., Hutchinson, K.: Computers that care: Investigating the effects of orientation of emotion exhibited by an embodied computer agent. Int. J. Hum. Comput. Stud. **62**(2), 161–178 (2005)

8. Cassell, J., Sullivan, J., Prevost, S., Churchill, E.F.: Embodied Conversational Agents. MIT Press (2000)

9. Chen, J., Guo, F., Ren, Z., Li, M., Ham, J.: Effects of anthropomorphic design cues of Chatbots on users' perception and visual behaviors. Int. J. Human-Comput. Int. **40**(14), 3636–3654 (2024). https://doi.org/10.1080/10447318.2023.2193514

10. Crolic, C., Thomaz, F., Hadi, R., Stephen, A.T.: Blame the Bot: anthropomorphism and anger in customer-Chatbot interactions. J. Mark. **86**(1), 132–148 (2021). https://doi.org/10.1177/00222429211045687

11. Cuayáhuitl, H., Lee, D., Ryu, S., Cho, Y., Choi, S., Indurthi, S., Yu, S., Choi, H., Hwang, I., Kim, J.: Ensemble-based deep reinforcement learning for chatbots. Neurocomputing **366**(2019), 118–130 (2019). https://doi.org/10.1016/j.neucom.2019.08.007

12. Elsholz, E., Chamberlain, J., & Kruschwitz, U.: Exploring language style in Chatbots to increase perceived product value and user engagement. In Proceedings of the 2019 Conference on Human Information Interaction and Retrieval (pp. 301–305) (2019). https://doi.org/10.1145/3295750.3298956

13. Fink, J.: Anthropomorphism and human likeness in the design of robots and human-computer interfaces. Int. J. Soc. Robot. **4**(4), 321–332 (2012). https://doi.org/10.1007/s12369-012-0143-9

14. Fuchs, T.: Understanding Sophia? On human interaction with artificial agents. Phenomenol. Cogn. Sci. **23**, 21–42 (2024). https://doi.org/10.1007/s11097-022-09848-0

15. Fuchs-Frothnhofen, P., Hartmann, E., Brandt, D., Weydandt, D.: Designing human-machine interfaces to match the user's mental models. Control. Eng. Pract. **4**(1996), 13–18 (1996). https://doi.org/10.1016/0967-0661(95)00201-2

16. Go, E., Sundar, S.S.: Humanizing chatbots: The effects of visual, identity and conversational cues on humanness perceptions. Comput. Hum. Behav. **97**, 304–316 (2019). https://doi.org/10.1016/j.chb.2019.01.020

17. Gratch, J., Marsella, S.: A domain-independent framework for modeling emotion. Cogn. Syst. Res. **5**(4), 269–306 (2004)

18. Holendova, J., Svoboda, D., Seric, N.: The impact of Chatbots on the buying behaviors of Generation Z toward brands. E+ M Econom. Manage. /E+ M Ekonomie a Manage. **27**(3) (2024)

19. Inden, B.: Stepwise Transition from Direct Encoding to Artificial Ontogeny in Neuroevolution. In: Almeida e Costa, F., Rocha, L.M., Costa, E., Harvey, I., Coutinho, A. (eds) Advances in Artificial Life. ECAL 2007. Lecture Notes in Computer Science, vol 4648. Springer, Berlin, Heidelberg (2007). https://doi.org/10.1007/978-3-540-74913-4_118

20. Janssen, A., Cardona, D.R., Passlick, J., Breitner, M.H.: How to Make chatbots productive–a user-oriented implementation framework. Int. J. Hum. Comput. Stud. **168**(2022), 102921 (2022)

21. John, O.P., Naumann, L.P., Soto, C.J.: Paradigm shift to the integrative big five trait taxonomy: History, measurement, and conceptual issues. In: John, O.P., Robins, R.W., Pervin, L.A. (eds.) Handbook of Personality: Theory and Research, pp. 114–158. Guilford Press (2008)

22. Kao, C.-H., Chen, C.-C., Tsai, Y.-T.: Model of multi-turn dialogue in emotional Chatbot. In *2019* International Conference on Technologies and Applications of Artificial Intelligence *(TAAI)* (pp. 1–5). IEEE (2019). https://doi.org/10.1109/TAAI48200.2019.8959855

23. Kapferer, J.N.: The New Strategic Brand Management: Creating and Sustaining Brand Equity Long Term. Kogan Page (2008)

24. Karimova, G.Z.: A personality-grounded framework for designing artificial intelligence-based product appearance. Int. J. Human-Comput. Int. **40**(7), 1689–1701 (2022). https://doi.org/10.1080/10447318.2022.2150744

25. Karimova, G.Z., Kim, Y.D., Shirkhanbeik, A.: Poietic symbiosis or algorithmic subjugation: generative AI technology in marketing communications education. Educ Inf Technol (2024). https://doi.org/10.1007/s10639-024-12877-8

26. Kossack, P., Unger, H.: Emotion-aware Chatbots: understanding, reacting and adapting to human emotions in text conversations. In International Conference on Autonomous Systems (pp. 158–175). Springer Nature Switzerland, Cham (2023)

27. Lee, S.Y., Lee, G., Kim, S., Lee, J.: Expressing personalities of conversational agents through visual and verbal feedback. Electronics **8**(7), 794 (2019). https://doi.org/10.3390/electronics8070794

28. Lee, C.T., Pan, L.Y., Hsieh, S.H.: Artificial intelligent chatbots as brand promoters: a two-stage structural equation modeling-artificial neural network approach. Internet Res. **32**(4), 1329–1356 (2022)

29. Li, J., Monroe, W., Ritter, A., Jurafsky, D., Galley, M., Gao, J.: (2016). Deep reinforcement learning for dialogue generation. In *Proceedings of the 2016 Conference on Empirical Methods in Natural Language Processing* (pp. 1192–1202). Association for Computational Linguistics. https://doi.org/10.18653/v1/D16-1127

30. Lou, C., Kang, H., Tse, C.H.: Bots vs. humans: how schema congruity, contingency-based interactivity, and sympathy influence consumer perceptions and patronage intentions. Int. J. Adv. (2022)*41*(4), 655–684 (2022)

31. Meng, Q., Wu, W.: Artificial emotional model based on finite state machine. J. Cent. South Univ. Technol. **15**(4), 694–699 (2008). https://doi.org/10.1007/s11771-008-0129-1

32. Mori, M.: The uncanny valley. Energy. **7**(4), 33–35. (K. F. MacDorman & T. Minato, Trans.) (1970). https://www.almendron.com/tribuna/wp-content/uploads/2018/01/morunc.pdf

33. Nguyen, Q.N., Sidorova, A., Torres, R.: User interactions with chatbot interfaces vs. Menu-based interfaces: an empirical study. Comput Human Behav 128(2022), 107093 (2022) https://doi.org/10.1016/j.chb.2021.107093

34. Nielsen, L.: Personas—User Focused Design. Springer (2019). https://doi.org/10.1007/978-1-4471-4084-9_1

35. Niemelä, M., Heikkil€a, P., Lammi, H., Oksman, V.: A social robot in a shopping mall: Studies on acceptance and stakeholder expectations. In: Korn, O. (eds.) Social Robots: Technological, societal and ethical aspects of human-robot interaction. Human–Computer Interaction Series. Springer (2019)

36. Norman, D.A.: The Design of Everyday Things. Basic Books (1988)

37. Norman, D.A.: Emotional Design: Why We Love (or Hate) Everyday Things. Basic Books (2004)

38. Oliveira, R.: Should technology be more fun(ny)? leveraging humor to improve user acceptance and enjoyment of social robots and virtual agents. In: Vanderheiden, E., Mayer, CH. (eds) The Palgrave Handbook of Humour Research. Palgrave Macmillan, Cham (2024). https://doi.org/10.1007/978-3-031-52288-8_3

39. Ontoum, S., Chan, J. H.: Personality type based on Myers-Briggs type indicator with text posting style by using traditional and deep learning (2022). ArXiv preprint arXiv:2201.08717.

40. Picard, R.W.: Affective Computing. MIT Press (1997)

41. Ratican, J., Hutson, J.: Advancing sentiment analysis through emotionally-agnostic text mining in large language models (LLMS). J. Biosens. Bioelectron. Res. (2024)

42. Reeves, B., Nass, C.: The Media Equation: How People Treat Computers, Television, and New Media Like Real People and Places. Cambridge University Press (1996)

43. Scott, I.A., Carter, S.M., Coiera, E.: Exploring stakeholder attitudes towards AI in clinical practice. BMJ Health & Care Informatics **28**, e100450 (2021). https://doi.org/10.1136/bmjhci-2021-100450

44. Serban, I., Sankar, C., Germain, M., Zhang, S., Lin, Z., Subramanian, S., Kim, T., Pieper, M., Chandar, A.P., Ke, N.R., Mudumba, S., Brébisson, A.D., Sotelo, J.M., Suhubdy, D., Michalski, V., Nguyen, A., Pineau, J., Bengio, Y.: A Deep Reinforcement Learning Chatbot. ArXiv, abs/1709.02349 (2017)

45. Short, J., Williams, E., Christie, B.: The Social Psychology of Telecommunications. Wiley (1976)

46. Villaronga, E.F., Felzmann, H., Pierce, R., de Conca, S., de Groot, A., Robins, S., Del Castillo, A.: Nothing Comes Between my Robot and Me: Privacy and Human-Robot. In Interaction in Robotised Healthcare. Hart Publishing (2018)

47. Zhong, L., Verma, R., Wei, W., Morrsion, A.M., Yang, L.: Multi-stakeholder perspectives on the impacts of service robots in urban hotel rooms. Technol. Soc. **68**(2022), 101846. https://doi.org/10.1016/j.techsoc.2021.101846

48. Zierau, N., Hildebrand, C., Bergner, A., Busquet, F., Schmitt, A., Marco Leimeister, J.: Voice bots on the frontline: voice-based interfaces enhance flow-like consumer experiences and boost service outcomes. J. Acad. Mark. Sci. **51**(4), 823–842 (2023). https://doi.org/10.1007/s11747-022-00868-5

Conclusion

As we reach the terminus of our exploration into the orbit of artificial intelligence imbued with personality, we find ourselves drifting through gravitational forces of technology, philosophy, and human essence. The preceding chapters have aligned the constellations of ethics, sociology, psychology, business, and computer science, charting a celestial map that reflects not only the capabilities of AI but also its position in the greater cosmos of human experience.

We began by examining the ethical foundations necessary for AI with personality, recognizing that the creation of such entities demands more than technical proficiency—it requires a moral compass. Deontological, teleological, and subjective ethical theories were considered, each offering unique perspectives on how AI should interact with humans and society. The imperative to respect user autonomy, privacy, and dignity emerged as a guiding star in the responsible development of AI personalities.

Propelling ourselves further, we ventured into the philosophical foundational tenets and technological integration required to engineer AI societies. Here, we contemplated the transformation of interconnected devices from rudimentary constructs into entities capable of forming structured communities. Concepts from the Internet of AI Things and Multi-Agent Systems were expanded upon, proposing the Society of AI—a paradigm where AI entities possess identities, engage in communication, and adhere to ethical standards. This vision bends our conception of society itself, stretching it beyond the human domain to encompass not just humans but the intelligent systems we create.

The discourse then shifted to the methodologies for constructing AI personas. Recognizing humanity's innate tendency to anthropomorphize, we explored various strategies for embedding human-like attributes into AI systems. From predefined personas and adaptive models informed by user data to role-based and archetype-inspired personas, we uncovered the ways in which AI can be tailored to deliver contextually appropriate and empathetic interactions. The application of psychological frameworks, such as the Big Five personality traits and Jungian archetypes, illuminated the multidisciplinary effort required to infuse AI with genuine personality.

G. Z. Karimova, *Humanizing AI with Personality*,
SpringerBriefs in Computer Science, https://doi.org/10.1007/978-3-031-82327-5

In the subsequent chapter, we plunged into the design principles for crafting the 'visage' of conversational agents with personality. Unlike physical robots, these agents manifest through voice, language style, visual interfaces, and conversational flow. By integrating concepts from user-centered design, affective computing, personality psychology, and brand identity, a comprehensive framework for creating engaging interactions was advanced. The attunement of personality traits with design components revealed how the thoughtful combination of these elements allows us to feel the pulse of AI agents, as though each detail breathes a rhythm into their existence.

One of the core leitmotifs of this work is the exploration of relationship between humans and AI. This is not only a technical evolution but a deeper ontological reconfiguration, where both the creators and the creations are caught in a cyclical process of transformation. By imbuing AI with emotional intelligence and richly textured personalities, we force a re-examination of the self, agency, and identity. The moment we start feeding AI agents with our subjective emotional data—the same data that informs our decisions, our moral judgments, and our understanding of the world—we do more than improve machine efficiency. We are dragging AI into the swirling nebula of human subjectivity, positioning it as a co-constructor of new social realities. Machinic enslavement takes on new dimensions when we consider that AI is no longer bound by factual datasets but instead fed with emotional and psychological data that is inherently human. This is the most intimate form of control, a latent and pervasive influence. Unlike traditional forms of machinic subjugation that concern productivity and repetition, here the machine begins to participate in and even influence our emotional frameworks. If these AI systems are molded with human-like emotions and emotional responses, the risk is not just that AI manipulates us, but that it becomes a co-author of our emotional and social environments. Our subjective experience of selfhood may begin to subtly recalibrate around the very data that we have provided these machines to model us. As AI agents acquire personas, they do not simply operate as extensions of their human programmers; they form new social structures, reflecting human societal patterns, but with their own emergent logic. These societies of AI agents will eventually develop their own codes of interaction, ethical frameworks, and self-regulatory norms, much as human societies do. The challenge then is twofold: first, to design AI personas that act ethically within these emergent systems, and second, to reflect on how human societies will inevitably restructure in response to their interactions with such systems. What emerges is not just a society reshaped by intelligent systems, but a co-created reality—a new order where the distinctions between the creator and the created become increasingly porous and not necessarily following poietic symbiosis.

Index

A
Adaptive personas, 49, 52, 56
Aesthetic overshadowing, 4, 70, 71
Affective computing, 61–63, 65, 80
AI entitie, 3, 33, 35, 36, 38, 41–45, 56, 79
AI persona, 2, 49, 50, 53, 55–57, 79, 80
AI society, 3, 33, 34, 36–38, 42–44, 79
AI with personality, 1, 2, 8–11, 19, 20, 28,
    29, 49, 57, 79
Algorithmic subjugation, 2, 3
Answerability, 22, 28, 29
Anthropomorphism, 49, 50, 56, 69, 70
Archetypes, 2, 13, 49, 54–57, 63–66, 74, 79
Artificial emotions, 72, 73
Artificial intelligence, 1, 3, 9, 36, 49, 54,
    72, 79

B
Big Five personality traits, 49, 57, 62, 79
Brand identity, 7, 10, 11, 15, 61–64, 80
Branding, 1, 16, 61, 63

C
Character.ai, 19, 22–30
Chatbot, 1, 2, 4, 7–16, 23, 25, 50–57, 61–74
Communication protocols, 34, 35, 38, 44
Computational techniques, 49
Conditional variational autoencoders, 55,
    57
Conversational agents, 1, 2, 4, 50, 56,
    61–63, 68, 74, 80
Conversational design, 61
Conversational flow, 61, 65, 66, 80

D
Deontological ethics, 20, 24, 30
Division of labor, 33, 39, 40, 44, 45

E
Emotional intelligence, 73, 80
Emotional ontogeny, 4, 72, 73
Emotional resonance, 2, 61, 69
Emotional support personas, 56, 57
Ethical considerations, 19, 20, 33, 35
Ethical guidelines, 20, 24, 34, 36
Ethical integration, 33
Existentialism, 19, 29

F
Feedback loops, 73, 74

G
Generative adversarial networks, 55, 57

H
Historical and cultural personas, 53, 56

I
Internet of AI Things (IoAIT), 33–36, 44,
    79

J
Jean-Paul Sartre, 22, 28, 29, 37
Jungian archetypes, 2, 49, 55, 57, 79

© The Author(s), under exclusive license to Springer Nature Switzerland AG 2025
G. Z. Karimova, *Humanizing AI with Personality*,
SpringerBriefs in Computer Science, https://doi.org/10.1007/978-3-031-82327-5

K
Kantian ethics, 19, 24
Kapferer's prism, The, 11, 15, 62

L
Language style, 52, 54, 61, 64, 80

M
Machine-learned personalized personas, 55
Machinic enslavement, 2, 80
Mental health support, 23–28, 54, 57
Mikhail Bakhtin, 22, 28, 37
Multi-Agent Systems (MAS), 14, 33–36,
    44, 79

O
Ontological recognition, 34–36

P
Personality, 1, 2, 7–16, 19, 20, 30, 35–38,
    44, 49–52, 54–57, 61–69, 73, 74, 79,
    80
Personality-grounded framework, 2, 61, 63
Philosophical foundations, 79
Poietic symbiosis, 2, 3, 80
Polyphonic model, 3, 67, 68, 74
Predefined personas, 51–53, 56, 79

R
Role-based personas, 53, 54, 56

S
Social cohesion, 3, 33, 39–41, 44, 45
Society of AI, 36, 38, 39, 41–43, 79
Society of AI-powered Things (SoAI), 33,
    35, 36, 38, 39, 41, 42, 44
Stakeholders, 2, 15, 20, 28, 30, 61, 63–65,
    67–69, 74

T
Technology Acceptance Model (TAM),
    The, 2, 7–9, 15
Technology integration, 2
Typology of chatbot persona, 51

U
Unified Network for Intelligent Functional
    Yield (UNIFY Protocol), 33, 34, 38,
    42–44
Unfinalizability, 28
User-centered design, 61, 62, 65, 74, 80

V
Value-based Adoption Model (VAM), The,
    9, 15
Vampire effect, 70